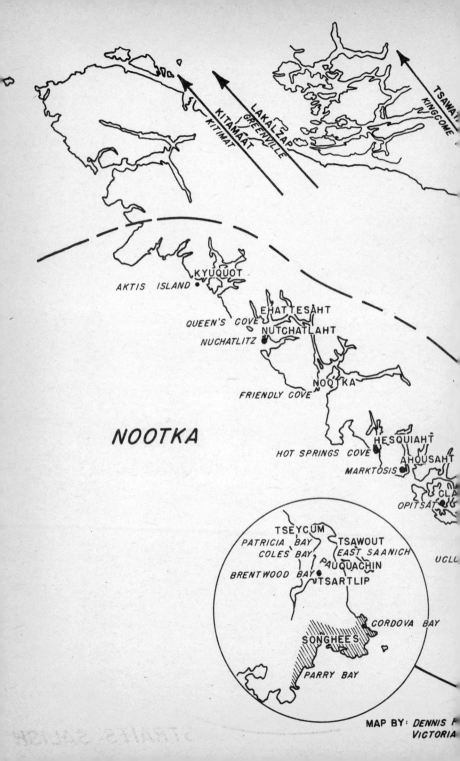

KITIMAT

KITAMAAT

LAKALZAP
GREENVILLE

TSAWAT
KINGCOME

KYUQUOT

AKTIS ISLAND

EHATTESAHT

QUEEN'S COVE

NUTCHATLAHT

NUCHATLITZ

NOOTKA

FRIENDLY COVE

NOOTKA

HESQUIAHT

HOT SPRINGS COVE

AHOUSAHT

MARKTOSIS

CLA

OPITSAT

TSEYCUM

PATRICIA BAY

TSAWOUT

COLES BAY

EAST SAANICH

PAUQUACHIN

BRENTWOOD BAY

TSARTLIP

UCLU

CORDOVA BAY

SONGHEES

PARRY BAY

MAP BY: DENNIS F
VICTORIA

STRAITS SALISH

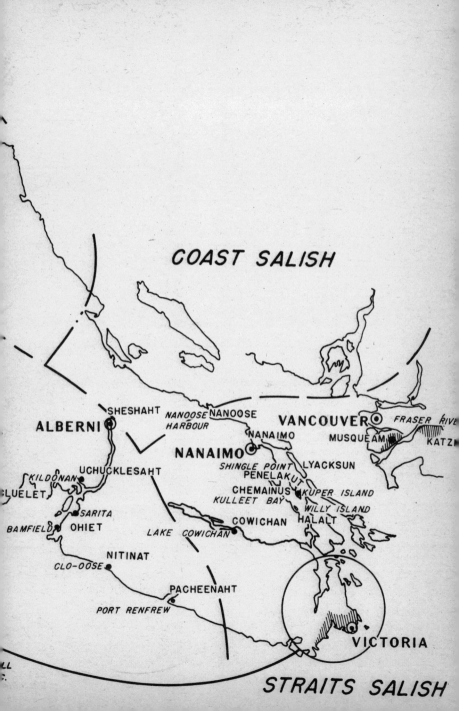

COAST SALISH

SHESHAHT
ALBERNI
NANOOSE *NANOOSE
HARBOUR
VANCOUVER ← FRASER RIVE
NANAIMO
MUSQUEAM
KATZ
NANAIMO
UCHUCKLESAHT
SHINGLE POINT
LYACKSUN
KILDONAN
PENELAKUT
LUELET
CHEMAINUS
KUPER ISLAND
SARITA
KULLEET BAY
WILLY ISLAND
BAMFIELD
OHIET
COWICHAN
HALALT
LAKE COWICHAN
NITINAT
CLO-OOSE
PACHEENAHT
PORT RENFREW
VICTORIA
STRAITS SALISH

Tales from the
LONGHOUSE

by Indian Children of
British Columbia

GRAY'S PUBLISHING LTD.
Sidney, British Columbia, Canada

SBN 0-88826-058-X

First Edition 1973

This Edition 1975

Printed in Canada

This book is dedicated to those
Native Indian people who proudly contribute
from their great heritage to
Canadians of every ethnic group.

The Mungo Martin Memorial Awards Fund,
B.C. Indian Arts and Welfare Society,
shall be the recipient of all royalties
and other monies obtained by the society
from the sale of this book.

Harriett E. A. Esselmont
Chairman Folklore Committee

ACKNOWLEDGMENTS

The Winspear Foundation for financial assistance with the publishing of this book.

Dr. George Clutesi for permission to use the drawing of the Longhouse which appears on the dust jacket.

Mr. Dennis Mitchell, graduate of Victoria Senior Secondary School 1967, with Drafting Instructor Mr. A. Eugene Frederick, for the production of the map which gives the locations of all represented Indian bands.

The classroom teachers in Indian Day and Parochial Schools and in the Provincial Elementary and Junior Secondary Schools who allowed time and evoked interest.

The contributing students who by painstaking endeavour searched for and wrote the stories of their people.

The B.C. Indian Arts and Welfare Society for its continuing interest in the younger generation of Native Indian people without which this book would not have been assembled.

The decorative petroglyphs which appear on pages viii, 10, 46, 52, 70, and 94 are reproduced from *Indian Rock Carvings*, published by Gray's Publishing Ltd., Sidney, British Columbia.

CONTENTS

FOREWORD

A number of years ago the members of the B.C. Indian Arts and Welfare Society decided to conduct an essay contest among Indian School children on Vancouver Island. It was agreed that many of the legends and much of the folklore of the Indians might disappear with the passing of the older generations, if steps were not taken before it was too late, to preserve both.

The first results of the contest were disappointing. The Indians the children wrote of, were those that they had seen on television or in the "movies". There was scarcely a mention made of Longhouses, dug-out canoes, the sea or whales, seals or salmon. All of which are an integral part of the life of the West Coast Indian. In time, however, and after persuasion, the essays began to change. It was obvious that the children were going to their elders for information and that they were being told some of the almost forgotten stories, customs and beliefs. Much of the material submitted was so interesting that the society felt it should be preserved—the present book is the result.

The book was written by children, but it is not intended to be read only by children. It is a form of verbal archaeology. As the palaeontologist and the archaeologist uses bits of bone and pottery to build up a picture of former civilizations, it is hoped that future students will find here bits of information that will help to build a more complete picture of Indian life on this coast.

It must be borne in mind that the Indian had no written language. These stories were never intended to be read. They were told by trained narrators and actors around a leaping fire in the centre of the Longhouse. The stories were told in the winter time, the play time for the Indians, for in the summer they worked hard to gather food and to prepare skins for clothing and furnishings. Against this background of fantastic shadows, occasioned by the swirling smoke as it rose towards the hole in the roof of the dwelling, of dark forests and of the sound of the crashing seas, it is easy to imagine how these stories slowly evolved. The Indian had an enquiring mind. He had to have a reason for everything, however imaginative that reason might seem to a more sophisticated mind.

This book represents an attempt by the young Indian of Vancouver Island to express their way of life, in writing, and in a language not their own.

In order to make the material more readily available to those who wish to use it for study purposes, the essays are arranged according to subject matter. Although no subjects were set under the contest regulations, children from different areas frequently selected the same one and it is interesting to compare the different versions of the same story. All the original essays are on file and may be consulted. The map of Vancouver Island shows the locations of the various Indian Bands whose stories were recorded by the children.

The members of the Folklore Committee, Mrs. Emma Hunt, Mrs. Mary Carr Travis, Mrs. Agnes Tate and the chairman Mrs. Harriett Esselmont derived great pleasure from the preparation of this book and will consider their efforts repaid if others share in the pleasure and interest.

Agnes Carne Tate

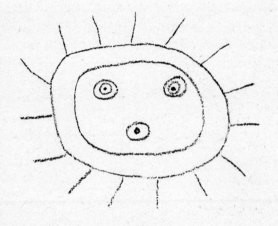

ORIGINS

In the Beginning

Jackie Pearl Albany. Age 13. Grade 8
Songhees Band
Craigflower School
Victoria, B.C.

The Legend of the Flood

Spencer Peters. Age 15
Ohiat Band
Gill Elementary Provincial School
Alberni, B.C.

First Honourable Mention, 1965

The Origin of the Vancouver Island Indians

Erma Modeste. Grade 10
Cowichan Band
Cowichan Senior Secondary School
Duncan, B.C.

The Halalt Tribe

Richard Thomas, Age 14. Grade 7
Cowichan Band
Kuper Island Residential School
Kuper Island, B.C.

Reward Through Peril

Stephen Charleson, Jr., Age 13. Grade 8
Hesquiaht Band
Christie Indian Residential School
Tofino, B.C.

1

The Stone-Heads

Yvonne Johnny. Age 15. Grade 9
Cowichan Band
Quamichan School
Duncan, B.C.

IN THE BEGINNING

Jackie Pearl Albany   Told by her mother

Long, long ago when the world was very young Nanabozo, the creator, as the Indians believed, found himself very much alone. There was nothing but water and air everywhere. He became very lonely. So as not to be alone he created the muskrat, beaver, and otter, but soon they grew tiresome as companions.

He wondered why he grew tired of their company. He decided he needed different creatures as companions. But there was too much water.

"The water is not solid enough," he said to himself. "I need something on which to rest my feet. I think that if I could stand on something solid, I could put one foot in front of the other and walk around."

After further thought, he tied his longest fishing line to the Muskrat, and told him to dive as deep as he could and try to bring something up from the bottom of the water. The muskrat was gone a long, long time, and when he finally came up he was so tired that he died. But Muskrat did not fail, because between his tiny paws was a little ball of mud.

Nanabozo took this little piece of mud and rolled it, and rolled it, and shaped it until it grew larger, and larger, and larger. When he was through rolling and kneading and moulding, the ball of mud was so large that thousands and thousands of creatures could live with Nanabozo as companions. Plants could grow and rivers could flow.

Being in such a hurry to create, Nanabozo left wet stretches here and there which will never be dry. These lands we know as muskeg.

Nanabozo could now rest happily and proudly because of his handiwork. He had more companions and he could put one foot in front of the other and move about the beautiful world which he had built.

THE LEGEND OF THE FLOOD

Spencer Peters   Told by his mother and grandmother

This is a story of the flood of Nitinat Lake and tells of mythical people, the Ya-ees. The Ya-ees lived in the days long passed, along the shores of Nitinat Lake.

This story is about one special winter when the rains never stopped. It seemed to rain forever. The lake rose higher and higher. The water came to the houses. Cha-uts-sem, the Chief, was afraid and his people were afraid. By now the water had reached into the houses.

Cha-uts-sem said to his people, "My children, the spirits tell me of a great flood that is about to overwhelm my people's land. Make strong ropes of the cedar branches. Load your belongings in your mighty canoes. Then tie your ropes to the roots of the elderberry, not the cedar or the hemlock trees because their roots do not go deep enough."

The people did not do as Cha-uts-sem requested. The people made their ropes fast. The ropes they made were weak. The people tied their ropes to the giant trees. The water rose and the wind blew so hard that some trees fell and broke the canoes and many people were drowned. But some people escaped the disaster. They drifted out to sea.

Cha-uts-sem, his wife and family had loaded their canoe with their goods. Cha-uts-sem called his canoe Klee-south. His canoe was six fathoms long. The chief Cha-uts-sem had made his own rope and had tied the rope to the roots of the elderberry. He tied the rope to the roots of the elderberry because the tree didn't overturn nor did the roots yield.

The water rose so that the tops of mountains could not be seen, save only one and that was Ka-Ka-Pay-Ya. On this mountain Kee-soulth sat. The Chief was asleep in his canoe. When he woke up, he saw a vision of the Great Tyee (a god) coming from the heaven. He took his seat in the bow and the Great Tyee said to sing this song four times. "Be good to me. Then I will not die." The Great Tyee told him that when he had sung this song four times the water would go down.

Cha-uts-sem, his wife and family left their canoe, Klee-soulth, on the top of Ka-Ka-Pay-Ya and returned to Nitinat Lake. The homes and the people were all gone. Ten days passed and Cha-uts-sem desired to find his people who had escaped from the disaster. Cha-uts-sem found some of his people half way between Jordan River and Sooke and others at Tatoosh, Neah Bay. Cha-uts-sem was glad to see his people.

Cha-uts-sem said to his people, "My canoe rests on Ka-Ka-Pay-Ya. Return with me to my village at Nitinat Lake. We will build a new village on the open beach." Cha-uts-sem called his village Dak-oo-acuts. It was a place of many dog-salmon. Every winter the Chief would climb Ka-Ka-Pay-Ya to see if Klee-soulth, the canoe was still there. They found everything the same as they had left it.

If you climb Ka-Ka-Pay-Ya, the mountain, you will find the water line that has been left from the Flood.

THE ORIGIN OF THE VANCOUVER ISLAND INDIANS

Erma Modeste

Many, many generations ago Tetusulthseam, (or god) sent down a man, named Decomet, and his stallus or mate. As time went on they got two daughters.

Years later, when the girls were young women, Decomet found out that Tetusulthseam had brought forth two more men, one named Secyulitshal, and his brother. There was also a dog named Secwakgus.

When Secyulitshal was brought forth he had with him a khulton, or pencil, but because he never made use of this pencil, it may be the reason why we cannot write our language.

Since Decomet and his stallus didn't know where Secyulitshal and his brother were, they got angry with their daughters because they said that they were the ones that should go to look for Secyulitshal and his brother.

These two girls therefore talked it over between themselves. From then on they started putting away seckala or dried fish one by one so their parents wouldn't know that they were taking it.

When they had enough for each one's pack they journeyed to find Secyulitshal and his brother. They started off by going over mountains until they were on top of Sallitsum which is now Bald Mountain.

It was from here that they saw the smoke from Secyulitshal's lealum or house. Then they walked along the top of this secmant or mountain, until they were in line with Secwakgus Secmant or Mt. Prevost. They then walked down the secmant and crossed the Cowichan Sectallo or River. They then crossed the Sectallo. Then started walking up Secwakgus Secmant. It was up this secmant that they found Secyulitshal's lealum, but no one was around when they arrived.

While cleaning the lealum they found two carved images of a woman. These two girls became jealous and burned the images. These images actually screamed when they were thrown into the fire. When Secyulitshal and his brother heard this scream, they ran to their lealum. When they arrived they found the two girls there. Secyulitshal and his brother accepted them as their stallus or mates.

As time went on they raised a lot of "mamana" or children. When they were all old enough Secyulitshal and his brother sent their "mamana" to seek for new homes. They were to spread out, as far as was possible. This is how the Indians of this Vancouver Island multiplied.

THE HALALT TRIBE

Richard Thomas   Told by his father

Once, many many moons ago, there was a very kind man. He lived in Saanich for a long time all by himself. He had not seen another person since his father had died of some kind of sickness. His mother had died a few hours after he was born.

From the time that he was only ten years old he knew how to hunt, carve, make weapons to kill animals, and how to make shelters for himself while out hunting. He knew how every animal looked and smelled. But he never knew what a woman looked like.

One day while out hunting he saw a strange creature walking around with two legs and two arms. It looked like himself, so he decided to capture it. He made the strangest trap. It was round on one side and was square on the other. It was big enough for a person to stand in. He saw that the creature came through the same part of the woods once every two days about when the sun is directly overhead. So he put the invisible trap on the trail just in time, for he could hear it coming. He ducked into some brush and waited. When he heard the creature scream he knew that he had caught it. Now he was able to get a better look at it and he noticed that it had the same features as he had. He wondered if it could speak. He spoke to it in his own language through a little round hole in the trap. To his surprise it answered him. He realized that this must be a woman. After a while he questioned her about her life. He found out that her parents also had died a few years ago.

The man decided to call his woman Halalt, after a beautiful fish that he had one day seen his father catch, because he thought that she too was beautiful. She decided to call him Michgin.

When they were very old they had many grandchildren. These young people wanted to call themselves the Michgins, but he said before he died, "This is Halalt's tribe."

There is still a tribe called Halalt. I know this, because I am one.

REWARD THROUGH PERIL

Stephen Charleson Jr.   Told by his great-uncle

It was a dark, stormy night, a squall was sweeping the coast. There was a downpour mingled with thunder, lightning and fog. Two men and two boys were struggling desperately in their puny dories, trying to avoid the numerous jagged reefs that dotted the coast. Each had earned a sufficient haul and had been rowing home when they encountered this storm. All day, they had expected it, but they never dreamt it would be this fierce. Hours of tedious rowing only took them farther and farther from their destination, Hesquiaht. The current they observed, was certainly strong.

The first to sight land through the thick fog was a husky man named Stephen; he yelled that, from his calculations, it was only a hundred yards ahead. Cautiously, avoiding the reefs, the dories triumphantly staggered into a calm, sheltered cove. It was like a dreamland; placid waters blended in with fragrant hemlock and stout cedar trees mixed with berry foliage of every description.

Along with all this, a small river full of fish gently made its way into the sea's calm depths; the hunting was excellent. It was an ideal place to live. So, they remained there long enough to patch up their dories and then set off for Hesquiaht on a calm, sunny morning. Reaching Hesquiaht they related their adventures, to the elders, who hearing of this new sheltered cove, decided to make it their new home, for their present homes, being located in the open, were constantly threatened by storms.

So, the Hesquiaht Indians gathered their possessions and moved into their newly discovered cove, which because it protected and sheltered them against the elements, they named Refuge Cove. Today it bears the name Hot Springs Cove because of the natural hot springs found there. Hot Springs, home of the Hesquiahts is a monument to those Indians who were brave and determined.

THE STONE-HEADS

Yvonne Johnny   Told by her grandmother

The first people that lived in the Cowichan Valley were the Stone-Heads. This race killed all baby boys and girls living then. All parents and children were killed, except one pregnant woman, who escaped and hid in the mountains.

A few weeks later she gave birth to her child in the mountains. Now having a baby boy, she called him Kissack meaning, "Knot".

The first day of his life, she dipped him into a spring, and he cried. Today the spring is called the "Cry Creek". During the night Kissack's mother camped at the Footprint Springs, now located at the Quamichan Reserve.

Years later, her son grew to be a boy of great strength and speed. His favourite sport was hunting. He liked hunting humming-birds, especially, and collected the feathers of these humming-birds and made a tunic out of them.

One of Kissack's adventures began while lying in the meadows, staring into the sky. He saw a big bird flying up above him. This bird was called the Golden Eagle. Wanting the bird very much, he returned home, and immediately carved a piece of bark into the appearance of his entrails. Days later, he laid himself on the ground and played dead, where the eagle could spot him easily. The eagle, seeing him, came gliding smoothly toward the ground, and tried to grab Kissack, but Kissack with great speed hit the huge eagle with a sturdy club, and killed it. He brought the eagle home to his mother. His mother, amazed, praised him. She plucked the feathers and used them to build a tee-pee to live in.

A few days later Kissack was exploring and found a strange looking race of people playing with a skull. They were kicking and throwing it back and forth to each other. These were the Stone-Heads.

Getting more information about these people from his mother, he wanted to get revenge. So after that day he went looking for the hardest kind of wood to make a strong club, hard enough to break a rock. He made his club out of iron wood, and sure enough, it broke a rock.

So the next day he returned to the camp of the Stone-Heads and they were playing the same game. Kissack hid behind a low bush and waited for the skull to roll his way. Finally the skull rolled toward the bush. With great strength and speed, he got his club and destroyed the heads of the men playing the game.

He then went to a building called the Big House, where many families lived, and killed all the Stone-Heads there.

Kissack returned to his mother and they were now able to leave the Tzouhalem Mountain, for Kissack had killed the Stone-Heads.

This story explains why there are no Stone-Heads living today.

POWER

Tsonoqua

Kenneth Charlie. Age 15. Grade 8
Cowichan Band
Kuper Island Residential School
Kuper Island, B.C.

First Prize, 1965

How the Stick Began

Johnny Peters. Age 15. Grade 7
Penelakut Band
Kuper Island Residential School

The Living Stick

Harry Peters, Age 13. Grade 8
Cowichan Band
Kuper Island Residential School

The Legend of the Squinilich

May Guerin, Age 13. Grade 8
Musqueam Band
Kuper Island Residential School

The Powerful Stick

Mary Ann Martin, Age 14. Grade 7
Cowichan Band
Kuper Island Residential School

A Person of the Most Power

Harvey Alphonse. Age 15. Grade 8
Cowichan Band
Kuper Island Residential School

Squanealach

Sandra Edwards. Age 15. Grade 8
Penelakut Band
Kuper Island Residential School

The Indian Doctor

Rita Underwood. Age 16. Grade 8
Tsawout Band
Kuper Island Residential School

Indian Dances

Alice Underwood. Age 14. Grade 7
Tsawout Band
Kuper Island Residential School

Second Prize, 1961

To Make an Indian Dancer

Rosemary Canute. Age 17. Grade 9
'No Band given
Kuper Island Residential School

Indian Dances

Sammy Wilson. Age 15. Grade 8
Cowichan Band
Kuper Island Residential School

Second Prize, 1965

Legend of Indian Dancing

Sandra Edwards. Age 14. Grade 7
Penelakut Band
Kuper Island Residential School

The Night of the Wolf

Ann Robinson. Age 12
Sheshat Band
Gill Elementary Provincial School
Alberni. B.C.

Indian Songs

Ernestine Wilson. Age 15. Grade 7
Cowichan Band
Kuper Island Residential School

TSONOQUA

Kenneth Charlie   Told by an elder

The worst of my days came when my grandfather, who at the age of one hundred and twelve lay on his death bed, suffering in agony from the pain in his old bones. It was a frightening day for everyone in our family. He told us of the visions that appeared to him while he awaited his death. Strange happenings that no one would believe.

He experienced these visions in his mind, for his old age had damaged his eyesight. As he explained these visions his words cut deep into my heart, to remain forever. I will never forget his words. He could hardly speak as he told us of these visions. He told us that there were spirits in the room but we could not hear or see them. "They are in here talking to me all the time," he said weakly, "But you have been unable to see them. Soon they will come to claim my spirit."

I could not bear the sadness of this moment, so I left my grandmother with him, alone in his room. I was not long out of the room when my grandmother came to me and told me that he wanted to see me in private.

Why would my grandfather want to see me in private? Would I be the one to inherit the strange powers that he had? Would I be able to do the work he had done? Or would I even have the power to heal the ill person? All these questions flashed through my mind as I walked slowly over to his bedside.

But these questions were answered when I stood next to his bed. For I saw him remove the Tsonoqua which was the source of power for my grandfather. It was made up of dried deer hooves. This necklace had powers which enabled my grandfather to heal ill persons.

I remember one time when my grandfather and other tribesmen had just arrived back in camp from a long fishing trip. My grandfather, not having very good meals on his trip, went to feast with the small group of men that he had with him. They gathered around the table quietly. After they had finished their meal they would tell the story of their journey over the rough seas, and speak of all the dangers that they had encountered.

My grandfather was not destined to get far in his speech, for just as he started he was interrupted by a crying woman with a baby in her arms. Sobbing loudly, she slowly opened the blanket and revealed the burnt-up body of her only child. The baby had been scorched by his grandmother's campfire.

She took the child to my grandfather to heal it, so it could live once again with its mother. My grandfather hesitating, took the child in his arms after a while, and walked to the Big House. Here I would witness whether or not the Tsonoqua did work. I watched him as he worked and talked to the spirits so that they could help him. This went on until the sun was ready to set. The door opened and my grandfather stepped out with a weary look and walked over to the mother. He told her that her child awaited her. This is one instance that I witnessed many years ago. Now my grandfather is old and weak.

Too much absorbed in thought I barely realized that he was slipping the Tsonoqua around my neck. He was telling me to carry on the work and not to fail to pass it on when my time comes or all the powers will be lost. I accepted the Tsonoqua with a fear that made me shake all over. With all the strength my grandfather had, he buckled the Tsonoqua on me. Finally he took his last breath and died with a weary smile on his face. By now the good spirit would have left my grandfather and entered into me.

HOW THE STICK BEGAN

Johnny Peters   Present Day Belief

The healing stick is a stick which finds a man's illness and takes out the evil in a person. There are two sticks but they are the same and they are supposed to have the same power. Here is how it began.

The stick started with a boy, a boy different from the rest of the boys in the village. He was raised by his grandfather who now was old in years. His grandfather said to him, "Go to the mountains, my son, and drink the water of the highest stream and you shall have a great power".

And so the boy went to the mountains, not knowing if it were true or not, but he did what his grandfather said. He went higher into the mountains and finally came to the top. There he saw the stream that he thought to be the highest. He got on his knees and drank as his grandfather had said. As he drank he felt good and powerful. He went back to the village. When he returned there was a sick baby and the medicine man was there but he was doing no good. The boy went over and said he could fix the little one, and the father said, "Go ahead". So the boy asked for food and fruit and ordered a fire built and he danced around the fire and threw the food in the fire. After he did this he went to the baby and rubbed him with his hands and went to the fire and threw the evil in the fire and the baby was better.

This went on for years and one day the man that was once a boy had become an old man. He was now ready to die and there were some people around who were his friends. He said, "Make two pieces of wood exactly the same." They did this. He was about to die and said more words and his last words were, "My power is in these sticks." He told someone to watch the sticks, and to throw food in the fire before using it. He said to use it for healing. So this they did and whenever they were needed they would take the sticks and heal a person or get rid of the evil spirits. And that is how the healing stick came to be. This stick is still used by our people in the Cowichan Valley.

THE LIVING STICK

Harry Peters   Told by his uncle

One night two years ago there was a gathering at a Big House on one of the reserves. The old Indian people, who are usually superstitious, brought a stick out into the middle of the hall. They said it had power and was able to move. One young man laughed at them and the stick just came out and knocked his hat right off his head. It had actually moved by its own power. A girl who did not believe it could move got pulled around. The stick came up to her and grabbed her somehow and she was dragged around in the Big House. When everybody saw this they were afraid. Nobody said then that they did not believe in it.

It was the first time it was brought into public for years and many people thought it was not true. Everyone now knew it was true for they had seen it.

The stick hasn't been seen since then. Maybe it has been destroyed. But I don't think so.

THE LEGEND OF THE SQUINILICH

May Guerin   A present day practice

The Squinilich is a piece of wood carved out in a face form with a mouth big enough for two hands. It leads two people around. If you are looking for a dead body it tells the people where the body is. It needs two men to hold it because it may go up, down, or anywhere. It crawls on the ground much of the time. The colour of it is red.

The origin of the Squinilich is that when a body from Cowichan was lost a god appeared to the people in Squinilich form and two men held onto it. The god led them through every move that the person had made before he died. Then it led them to the body.

When the Squinilich is passing by the people the men must take off their hats or the Squinilich will knock their hats off their heads. You must believe in the Squinilich in order that it may use its power.

THE POWERFUL STICK

Mary Ann Martin   Told by her mother

Long ago before any man could be a witch doctor he had to learn many things and how to work wonders. This man of forty-six was the witch doctor of his tribe. This man had carved something that looked like a board with a picture of a face on it. It was painted dark red. After the witch doctor had finished carving, drawing, and painting the picture he put some of his power in the stick and put it away in a box. Then one of the big dances came up. So the witch doctor took the board out and asked for four men to hold it, one on each side where the holes were. Then the witch doctor started to beat on the drum, and to sing a song. Right away the stick started to dance and at the end of the dance the witch doctor took it, just as my mother told me.

When you take hold of this stick, it is said that you can't let go until the stick stops, even if you try to let go, your hands hold on. At the big dance I went to last year the four men that were holding it were about four or five inches off the ground, while the stick was dancing. I know even today it is in the Big House, because it was set free by the witch doctor at the big dance two or three weeks ago at Kuper Island.

A PERSON OF THE MOST POWER

Harvey Alphonse

At a big dance in Duncan, the Indian dancers have what they call a Squeneelech.

First of all they start by placing blankets on the ground in one place with two pieces of wood about fourteen inches long and nine inches across. There are two pieces of this wood and both have holes in them where the men can grab hold to start the Squeneelech. Food is placed on the blankets and later is burned.

While the food is being burned, two men grab one block and they are dragged around the fire. These pieces of wood have a spirit in them.

At the bottom row of spectators the four men are dragged from person to person. They find out the person with the strongest power by the men being stopped by the blocks of wood in front of a certain person.

At one big dance it was a woman who had the power to find a drowned man. Two other women had to hold her back. Even then she was not slowed down much. The four men were dragged around the fire. Then the Squeneelech ended its movements for that night.

The Squeneelech is used in all the Cowichan Big Houses. Our people believe in the spirit of the Squeneelech.

SQUANEALACH

Sandra Edwards

Long ago people across on the American side created the Squanealach party.

One day one of the band went down to the beach and found there two strange pieces of board which he brought to the Chief. The Chief listened to the boards and as he listened he seemed to hear someone speaking. As soon as he heard this he told the important men of the tribe. All the people of the American tribe think these two pieces of board are very sacred, so they keep them with their sacred possessions. The boards are square but they have two big holes in them where one man holds the Squanealach with both his hands and another holds the board with one hand and with the other he holds the first man on the back.

When the American people get to the dances, sometimes they are asked to perform ceremonies with these boards. The people say that the boards tell the man where a body is, when no one is able to find it. The men who hold the boards must believe in it or the boards will not co-operate.

The American people keep the Squanealach as a sacred possession because of the power that it has. The word Squanealach means power. The men and the boards together may do many great things which no one would believe until they have had the proof by seeing it for themselves.

THE INDIAN DOCTOR

Rita Underwood   Told by her mother

This legend is told by our forefathers. It tells how a man would become an Indian doctor and help his people. It is said that a young girl wanted to help her people but she was not to become an Indian doctor because the Indians said that she was here only to work and to give new life. A young man, pure and not married was chosen. He would stay one half-moon with the wisest of his tribe, who would tell him everything that he would have to endure and the things that he himself must do. Then at the time of the full moon the young man was left with only a knife. He was instructed to go to the mountain, where many eagles lived.

On his way there he was tempted. He saw a young Indian maiden. She called to him. But he knew it was a witch doctor who did not do good and did not want anyone else to do good either. So the young man kept on. He could see many things that were pleasing to the eye, but he did not allow anything to distract him.

He was to stay up the mountain three years. There, during those years he would kill, clothe and cook for himself. He was to be on his own with only a knife. During those years he would pray to the spirits, to help him. Later on the plants would talk to him and tell him what they were used for. He would study what he was told. After the three years he was to kill three eagles and to take the feathers and make a hat. He then would start down the mountain. Again he would be tempted.

If he yielded to the temptation he would become an evil witch doctor and would kill instead of healing.

It all depended on the young man himself, as to what he would become.

INDIAN DANCES

Alice Underwood

Many countless moons ago when the white snows came, the Indians from all over the Reserve would gather in the Big House. There they would build two big fires to keep out the cold. Day and night the braves put wood on the fires and kept them burning brightly, to keep the cold away from their wives and papooses.

At night time just as the moon came up over the mountains, the Indians would dance around the fires and the children would sit at the back watching the big ones dance.

Each year a new dancer would be grabbed. He would be put to bed in a far-off corner of the Longhouse while the wives would make his hat and cloak. After this was done they would stand the new dancer on his feet, dress him, and at night he would dance.

One night an old Indian Chief spoke in a strange tongue. He spoke thus, "I, Chief Thunderbird, command a new dancer to go into the air." Then he spoke privately to the new dancer. And the dancer flew into the air. He even went over the fire. He came down again swift of foot and strong of muscle. Everyone·in the Big House wondered, but no one dared to ask.

Then in summer when all the Indians left the Big House, old Chief Thunderbird died. The dancer became the next chief and was named Chief Great Eagle.

Once again the Indian people went to the Big House. This time when the new dancer was grabbed it was Chief Great Eagle who spoke the strange words and again the Indian dancer was able to go into the air. And just as did Chief Great Eagle, the dancer became more swift and more powerful in strength, when he returned to the ground.

This went on for many moons. Even now the dancers continue around the big fires. But no one remembers the words to send the dancers into the air. The words were lost during the years. We know that this happened long ago because our parents tell us the tale.

TO MAKE AN INDIAN DANCER

Rosemary Canute

The Indian dances were originated by old people who lived long ago.

These dances were handed down to other Indians. The dances are still going on today. An Indian dancer is chosen by a former dancer.

Six or eight men are chosen to grab the new dancer. After he is grabbed he is put into a tent made out of four blankets. This tent is in the Big House. On the first day six or eight men lift the new dancer up. But if the dancer is a woman or girl, women lift her up.

The grabbers lift the dancer, then bite, as they lift him up higher. They blow on his sides where they have bitten him. If he doesn't holler on the second day they will try the same thing again, but if he still doesn't yell, one of them will use the deer hoofs, which are attached to a wooden handle. These are heated and used on the back of the dancer until he does holler.

On the fourth day one of the men will take the dancer out of the tent and shake him around the fire, then take him back to where they started from. Then another does the same thing until it gets to the last grabber. He takes him back into the tent.

Early next morning this new dancer takes a bath, after which he puts on his costume. He is to run outdoors every morning.

During the four days he is actually on a diet. He is not supposed to have a full meal. He eats half of each food prepared. The tea or coffee is always lukewarm, not any warmer. He uses a straw to drink.

Towards the end he doesn't wear his hat or costume, he wears an ordinary kerchief around his head with his eyes covered. During the time he has spent since he was first grabbed he has probably learned a great deal.

Some of the old people will have given him or her lectures, especially if the dancer is young. If the dancer is older then he is given only a few of the more important talks. This new dancer is not allowed to make up another song until after four years have passed.

It now takes a lot of money to make a new dancer compared with what it did in the old days. They take up collections from all the people who have been invited.

The blankets that were used for the tent are given away to a special person.

Usually an Indian name is given after a person has become a dancer. The rules for those who become dancers are not as strict as they used to be. But only those who have been recommended by an older person will be grabbed to become a dancer.

Usually it is the person who has not been good. The new dancers learn a lot. The dancer may change a little from what he was by taking the lectures from the older people.

INDIAN DANCES

Sammy Wilson   Told by his mother

The Indians will never forget what their ancestors danced for; nor how they were led to the Big House to dance. The chief of the tribe knew how the dancers would dance. He also knew how to make them dance. He himself used to dance for weddings or good hunting or to cure the sick.

In the spring of every year the chief would gather all his braves into the Big House. There they would perform many dances. The dancers wore a costume and carried deer hooves on a stick.

Before dancing they would shake the stick, which would make a rattling sound. After shaking this they would hand the stick to the person looking after them. Then they would start to dance. They would dance around the fire and the drums would beat out the steps of the dancer. This kept up, until one year the rain didn't come and the crops were bad. The chief told his tribe to be calm. He also told them that he was going up the mountain to pray to the rain gods.

The chief climbed high up Mount Prevost. A dark cloud covered all the land of the Cowichan Band. There was lightning all over. As the chief climbed he was struck by a lightning bolt.

The chief was out so long that a group of braves set out for him. They were nearing the foot of Mount Prevost when they saw their chief lying on his back. He was dying, so he sent the youngest of the braves to gather herbs. This of course was an excuse, for the chief wanted to make plans.

The chief wanted to grab this youngest brave as an Indian dancer. So the chief told the other braves how they were to grab the young brave. So when he came back with the herbs the others grabbed him as the chief had told them to. Then they placed him on the ground and bit at his stomach. Then they tickled him. This made him shout. Then after they were finished they made him sit down and make up a song. After he finished his song he danced to it.

Then the whole tribe learned his song and added drums. These dances were held outdoors under the open sky. Not long after they built a large house which is now called the Big House. The new dancers have to stay in this Big House for a few weeks. All this time they do not take off their costumes. They bathe in cold water every day. The dancers do all these things when they are grabbed to become Indian dancers.

The new dancers dance each night till there is a big dance. All the new dancers dance at this big dance. When you become a dancer you have to put up a dance and invite the other dancers to the dance. After the dance you have to give out sugar or dishes or blankets. These remind the people that their ancestors danced for the food and clothing that they got.

They also dance in thanksgiving for the year of good crops. Every year people gather together for a big dance. Each year there are new dancers. These things are still carried on in the Big House today. The dances are held during the spring of the year.

LEGEND OF INDIAN DANCING

Sandra Edwards

Long ago people started grabbing men or women and this custom has been carried down from the ancestors of the Indians today. The men tell the boy or man whom they are to grab, to go down to the Big House, because they are going to hold a meeting. When everybody is at the Big House they tell them which person they are going to grab, and instruct them to be ready when he or she comes in.

When the person gets in they tell them to sit down and wait for someone to speak. The man waits for a long time. Then they jump him, before he can move. Then some men go and help to lift him up. As they are holding the person they put a kerchief on his head to cover his eyes. If he fights they will bite him and hold him tight, until he can't move. If he does not fight they will blow on him, on his stomach, sides and neck. They go around the fire for an hour blowing and biting him. While they are doing this some women fix the bed where they are to lay him down. They lay him down and cover him up. After they lay him down they ask a boy who is not a dancer to look after him. The boy goes and lies beside the man and gets him anything he wants. Then the people who grabbed him get three blankets and hang them around his bed. They call it a tent. They blow him up for four nights. If he hollers on the fourth night they will sing his song.

During the four nights four men go to his bed and blow him up. On the fifth night they will have him sitting up with a blanket wrapped around the lower half of his body. Then the four men who were blowing him up will go and grab him. One will take his right arm, another will take his left, one more will take his head and the last one will hold his waist. They'll shake him and sit him down. When he is sitting down he sings his song, then dances around the fire. After he is finished they will lay him in the bed. The next morning they will make a place where they put a tub and sit him in it. Someone stands on a chair and splashes water on him.

Before the men do all this they get four boys who are not dancers to do the Scotch Dance. The boys wear paint and a hat. First they grab the buckets, next they take the ferns, then the sticks and lastly the rocks. After the four boys are prepared they start dancing. Then the men tell them to sit down. They do the Scotch Dance for four years. When the fourth year is up they are grabbed.

After the Scotch Dance, the men who grabbed the boys will put new clothes on him and start making his hat. In the night time they shake his costume and put it on him. The next day he visits his relations and receives his lectures. The lectures they give will help him to become more mature. They give him a straw to use when he drinks and a wooden fork for his scratcher. Most of the old people give him lectures to help him and to make him understand about the dancing. He wears his costume for the first year, and he carries his stick.

All the other years that he dances, from the time he is taken until he dies, he does not wear his costume. It is burnt or given away.

THE NIGHT OF THE WOLF

Ann Robinson   Told by her mother

On the night of the full moon the Leghorn tribe was to hold the customary dance of the wolf for the wolves were believed to be the ancestors of these people.

They wore nothing but a wolf skin over their bodies. These men were rubbed in the fat of a wolf and they crawled on their hands and knees as if a wolf.

To wise old Augashmit there was something especially exciting about this night, as if something unexpected was about to happen. He told the men to beware of the evil that lurked nearby. They said that nothing must prevent their native custom from being kept up.

They dressed as usual and crawled around a large fire giving frightful wolf cries. Suddenly one of the men gave a gasp, for a real wolf had slipped into the ring and was giving the same frightful cries. Another one appeared and joined the ring. Luckily it was just two males that heeded the calls. No one would get up to leave the circle for fear the wolves would attack. They all had to keep up their cries and their crawling. Even though they were so tired that they could hardly crawl they had to keep it up, for their lives depended upon it.

At dawn the wolves left and the men went home to tell of their adventure, but they found that they could not talk for their voices were weak from all the howling. When they regained their voices they told of the adventure, which is now told and handed down from father to son.

From that time on they consulted Augashmit, the chief, before going out to their worshipping grounds.

This legend has been told for many generations by my ancestors, and this is as it was told to me.

INDIAN SONGS

Ernestine Wilson   Told by her mother

An old Indian of long ago revealed to the people how an Indian began chanting songs in the Indian language.

It was only by accident that this happened. He was walking through the woods and became weary, so he lay down under a tree where he fell asleep. While asleep strange dreams came to him in the form of Indian songs. He dreamed that a story was being told to him and that this story could be sung in the Indian language and that it would have meaning for the Indian people. When he awoke, he too was singing.

When he arrived at the Indian village the people stared at him. They asked him what he was singing about. He shrugged his shoulders and told them to go to the woods and to lie down under the tree that had its bark peeled halfway up. An Indian tried it and he too had this same dream. When he returned to the Indian settlement he also was singing. These songs have meaning for the one who sings them and for the very old Indians.

NATURE

Why the Wind Moans
During the Hours of Winter

Michael Wilson. Age 12. Grade 5
Cowichan Band
Kuper Island Residential School
Kuper Island, B.C.

The Legend of the Lightning

Johnny Jack. Age 18. Grade 8
Cowichan Band
Kuper Island Residential School

The Legend of the Lightning

Joan Sam. Age 16. Grade 8
Cowichan Band
Kuper Island Residential School

The Thunder

Tony Bob. Age 18. Grade 8
Cowichan Band
Kuper Island Residential School

The Legend of Mr. Raven the Imitator

Georgina Pointe, Age 15. Grade 7
Nanaimo Band
Quennel Provincial School
Nanaimo, B.C.

WHY THE WIND MOANS
DURING THE HOURS OF WINTER

Michael Wilson   Told by his grandfather

Many moons ago the Chief's son was awakened from his sleep by a strange noise. He thought it was the sound of his necklace with the bear claws on it. But the sound he heard was a shivering, cracking sound and the wind was moaning through the trees.

He left his tent and outside he saw a set of teeth hanging. Some of the teeth were broken and others were lying on the ground.

The wind moaned harder and it asked in its most pleading voice, "Please mend my teeth. Put them back in place and I will reward you." The boy understood the voice of the wind. So as the wind howled and raged the boy worked to put the teeth back in the wind.

The wind did not forget this kindness and when summer comes he gives us the soft breezes to cool the lands and to whisper to us in the leaves of the trees.

THE LEGEND OF THE LIGHTNING

Johnny Jack   Told by his grandfather

There was a boy whose parents used to tell him that if he wanted to obtain spiritual powers he was to bathe in the rivers and lakes. If there were spirits there during the time that he was taking his bath, they would surely enter into him.

One day during the rainy season he went to his usual swimming place. Suddenly the power came over him. though the boy himself did not realize this.

28

He started for home and as his friends saw him coming, like any other boys, they teased him to make him angry. Unknown to himself he closed his eyes in anger and as he opened them again suddenly lightning struck one of the boys he was looking at and the child died. When the boy got home he began to wonder why the lightning had not struck him, but he could not find the answer to his question.

The next time he went out to bathe he questioned the spirits. Finally he was given the answer in the song that he was to sing when he was making the lightning. From that time on he had the power to make lightning but each time that he got angry he caused a death of a person.

In time the men who had power to see the spirits in another person were asked to search out this boy. Everyone assembled in the Longhouse to plan how they might search for this killer.

After they picked him out they planned to kill him. First they took him far from their own village. Here they beat him and put him in a canoe and started out for another part of the Island. On the way the boy gradually freed himself from the ropes that bound him. The men did not notice this for they thought that he was safe enough. The only thing that really bothered them was the tape around his eyes, for they feared that the boy would cast the lightning upon them and kill them all if the band were removed from his eyes.

When the boy had worked himself loose he jumped out of the canoe and began to run across the top of the water. In trying to run away he tried not to open his eyes for he feared the men with him might get struck by lightning and he meant no harm to them. He could not help it when he had cast lightning on the boys in the village but at that time he had not learned to control his powers. The men tried to prevent him from escaping by shooting at him with bows and arrows but they could not get him because he was too fast for them. When he had finally got far from them he opened his eyes there was a flash of lightning. So as you look up in the sky on a rainy day you will see where and how far he has travelled by the flashes of lightning that streak across the sky.

They say that this is how the lightning was brought to Vancouver Island. Whenever it rains the boy starts to run again for he likes to feel the rain upon him. But he is no longer hunted down. Each time the Indians see the lightning they keep their children indoors for they fear death when the lightning strikes.

THE LEGEND OF THE LIGHTNING

Joan Sam   Told by her grandmother

Once, long ago in a dark desolate forest dwelled a band of Indians whose houses stood along the shores of the roaring Twasis.

Here ruled a wise old Chief who had rightly won the love and respect of his people. As the years passed, his tribe's love for him grew stronger until one day, assembled in their chief's house, they saw their leader breathe his last breath. At that same moment, as his spirit left his body, there came forth a whistle of the wind, a clap of thunder and gigantic bolts of lighning, which struck the earth with tremendous force.

The Chief was happy to go but he sorrowed to see his tribe mourn over the loss of their leader and he wept tears that came down as torrents of rain.

From that day forth, Indians, whose faces were accustomed to be wreathed in smiles were solemn, seldom to smile nor to express emotion.

To this day Indians believe that when an Indian dies and the spirit goes to the creator, bolts of lightning and torrents of rain descend as a sign that even though gone in body the person still is with their loved ones in spirit, and will come to visit the earth in the form of lightning.

THE THUNDER

Tony Bob   Told by his mother

This story commenced when the chief ordered all the baby boys to be killed, because there was a giant that took them and he didn't want the babies to be taken by the giant. But the mother of one child hid her son. She took him away from the village and roamed around so that their whereabouts should not be known.

As the time went by the boy grew big and strong, and he began to play about. Then his mother made him a bow and arrow to hunt for little birds. And from all the little birds that he killed he took the skin and made himself clothes. Soon he had enough for a whole outfit, and he put it on and went through the woods hunting for his food. When the giant Thunder saw the clothes, he wanted them for himself and he chased the boy. The boy ran and hid from Thunder. He told his mother about this and she told him that Thunder lived on Mount Tzuhalem, but just where nobody could be sure.

As the boy grew he wanted to find the place where Thunder dwelled. So he tried to be as great as Thunder. His mother wanted to help him to fly like Thunder. But as they were walking along Thunder struck his mother and she turned into a rock. The boy sprinkled medicine on his mother. Then he started to fly again and his mother ran after him. Then Thunder struck again. His mother fell to the ground a second time, and again the boy went back to help his mother. Just as they started up the creek Thunder struck the third time. This time the boy could not help his mother because he had used up all the medicine. So the boy left his mother there. To this day the Indians say that she is the big rock that stands beside the creek that flows into Quamichan Lake.

If you spit three times beside the rock and dip your hook three times in the creek before you fish, you will be sure to catch a trout.

The Thunder kept on chasing the boy until they came to Quamichan Lake. There Thunder struck the boy and he fell beside the little island that stands in the lake, near to the big rock.

The Indians say that when the water rises the rock also rises and the rock can sometimes be seen alongside the island.

THE LEGEND OF MR. RAVEN THE IMITATOR

Georgina Pointe   Told by her mother

Aut-oosh-mit always had his little canoe with him. He was always planning some mischief.

One evening he was rowing around in the fog in his little canoe. He was talking to himself.

He said, "Where are you going? Where are you going? Are you lost?" And he laughed to himself.

"No, I know where I am." he told himself. "All I have to do is to open up the fog to see where I am."

Mr. Bear and Mr. Raven heard little Aut-oosh-mit from where they were on the shore.

Mr. Raven said, "Let's have a little fun with Aut-oosh-mit". And they would call to him, "Over here! Come over here."

And Aut-oosh-mit would ask, "Who is there?" And they would answer, "Only your echo."

But Aut-oosh-mit started rowing towards the voice on the shore.

As he came near he noticed a bright light from a bonfire. Here he saw Mr. Bear and Mr. Raven. "What are you doing?" he asked. "Oh, we are just getting warm," they replied.

Aut-oosh-mit laughed when he saw Mr. Bear warming his hands at the fire with the grease dripping into the fire from his hands. Mr. Raven was holding his hands to the fire also but his hands were becoming skinny and dry.

"The joke is on you Mr. Raven," cried Aut-oosh-mit. "It was you that imitated me while I was in the fog, and now you are imitating Mr. Bear. But you'll never imitate anyone again. Look at your hands. They are becoming shrivelled and dry while Mr. Bear's are still fat and greasy."

And Aut-oosh-mit left Mr. Bear rolling around on the ground laughing at Mr. Raven the imitator.

CUSTOMS AND WAYS OF LIFE

Finding Food

> Harvey Alphonse, Age 14, Grade 7
> Cowichan Band
> Kuper Island Residential School
> Kuper Island, B.C.

How the Indians Made the Things They Needed

> Marie George, Age 9, Grade 3
> Cowichan Band
> St. Catherine's School
> Duncan, B.C.

The Last Hunt

> Eileen Charleson, Age 14, Grade 8
> Hesquiaht Band
> Christie Indian Residential School
> Tofino, B.C.

Life of the West Coast Indians

> Sheila Cooper, Age 13, Grade 7
> Tsartlip Band
> Brentwood School
> Brentwood Bay, B.C.

Making Oolichan Oil

> Lois Dawson, Age 13, Grade 7
> Tsawataineuk Band
> Kingcome Inlet Indian Day School
> Kingcome Inlet, B.C.
>
> *Second Prize, 1966*

Canoe Pulling

Rosemary Wilson. Age 16. Grade 8
Tsawout Band
Kuper Island Residential School

The Legend of the Lovers

Pearl Wilson. Age 16. Grade 7
No Band Given
Kuper Island Residential School

The Two Brothers

Regina Charlie. Age 16. Grade 8
Clayoquot Band
Opitsaht Indian Day School
Tofino, B.C.

Olden Days About Indians

Marion E. Peter. Age 12. Grade 4
Ucluelet Band
Ucluelet Indian Day School
Ucluelet, B.C.

Spirit Finders

Edith Pelkey. Age 13. Grade 7
Tsawout Band
Kuper Island Residential School

Third Prize, 1964

An Indian Legend

Roseanna Charlie. Age 13. Grade 7
Penelakut Band
Kuper Island Residential School

Second Prize, 1962

34

FINDING FOOD

Harvey Alphonse

The Indians of long ago got their food by using implements such as bows and arrows, spears and snares. The bows and arrows were used for big animals such as deer, bear and cougar. If at any time an Indian had no spear he used the bow and arrow. Today the gun is taking the place of the bow and arrow, for it is a more powerful weapon.

The spear is used to catch fish. At the end of the spear is tied a string so that when the spear is thrown it can be pulled back. The spear is thrown by hand. The spear gun has taken the place of the ordinary spear. When using a spear gun you need only to pull a trigger. The ordinary spear is still used most often by the Indians.

The snare is another method used by the Indians. Over the years it has been much improved. The snare was mostly used to catch small animals such as rabbits, squirrels and mink. A thin rope is needed for the snare. Traps are now used to catch these small animals. Big traps are used to catch the bear, and the wolf and other large animals. The traps were used, not to kill the animals, though some of them died because they were held so long. in pain and without food.

HOW THE INDIANS
MADE THE THINGS THEY NEEDED

Marie George   Told by her mother

Long ago the Indians used to take a tree and after they had chopped it down they would take off the outside bark and use it for a canoe. They would chop deep into the cedar tree as they shaped the canoe.

They would go to the beach to catch seafood. When they came home they ate the seafood with utensils made from cedar wood. Large spoons were made from horn. Cups and plates were carved from the cedar wood.

The Indians used to go to the mountains and get a root which was sweet. They made sugar and tea from the plants which they found.

For clothes the Indians used deer skin. When it was cold in the winter they would kill the deer and skin it. Then the skin was cleaned and dried, after which it was made into clothes. In the summer time the clothes and even the shoes were made from cedar bark. In order to make these things the cedar bark was smoothed until it was very thin. Then it could be made into any shape that was wanted.

The houses were made from cedar logs and planks. Woven rugs and room dividers were made from cedar bark or animal skins.

The Indians planted wheat and made flour from it.

For their trinkets and necklaces and bracelets they gathered tiny sea shells.

THE LAST HUNT

Eileen Charleson   Told by her aunt

In a remote and peaceful village there once lived a mighty Kwakiutl Chief. Now it was said of this leader that he was a great hunter. One sombre day, when winter was fading into spring, Klee Wyck, the Chief, set out on an unusual hunt. Unusual because no brave ventured out in the winter. But Klee Wyck's people were in desperate need of food, and to him the needs of his people always came first. Stealthily he crept through the forest, alert of every sound. Hours passed, and through the heavy grey mist, he sighted a deer. Cautiously, he crept towards it, not realizing that at the same moment, another desperate hunter, a woman, pursued the same animal. According to custom, women were forbidden, under penalty of death, to hunt.

Fearing that she would be discovered, the woman shot at Klee Wyck and left him there to die.

When, after several moons the Chief did not return to his village, the councillors prepared a search party, and set out to find him. Sadly they returned to their camp the next morning, chanting a plaintive hymn. Klee Wyck, their mighty Chief, was dead. Reverently they placed his body in a beautifully carved coffin and set it on top of a pole, facing their majestic green forest.

There it remains to this day. It is said by his people that Klee Wyck's spirit leads them in all their hunting expeditions.

LIFE OF THE WEST COAST INDIANS

Sheila Cooper   Told by her father

When the Indians lived on their own, they used to live a sort of care-free life. They lived in Longhouses made out of big cedar slabs, and they used wooden pegs for nails. This is where they stayed during the winter and where they would keep all their provisions for the winter months.

When spring comes, everyone starts to get ready to move. When the weather gets warm enough they return to their hunting grounds where they have been going for many past years. Here they hunt for their meat for winter. They used to dry it and store it away. All the hides were dried and saved for their own use. The women used to shred cedar bark and dry it for some of their clothing. Also the women used to dig certain kinds of bulbs for potatoes and these were also dried. They would dry berries in slabs and when they used it they would just soak it in water. It was called pemmican. After all these months they would do all this, just taking their time. No one rushed, for there was always plenty. The men used to make canoes out of cedar logs by chopping and hollowing out a single log. The paddles were made as well. Another thing the men used to do was kill the wild goats and the women used the hair for blankets. This hair was spun and braided, and it made a very heavy and warm blanket.

So now, running into fall, they would return to their Longhouses. Here several families lived together. Then they would get the fish, just when they first went up the river to spawn. And they smoked it. But they always shared with each other. That's why they always say about an Indian giver, "He always wants to get something back in return for what he gives." But that is how they always worked it, and in that way no one ran short of food to eat. But now, if we were to try and live that way, we just couldn't, for everything has changed.

MAKING OOLICHAN OIL

Lois Dawson

First of all we put a net up or down the river, as long as the net is under water. Wherever we put the net, the current in the water has to be strong, so that the oolichans can swim into the net. The net we use is called the "ta-galth".

The net "ta-galth" has very tiny holes in it, and is used mainly for catching oolichans.

We measure the oolichans by the tubsful. We have to get a couple of hundred tubsful of oolichans. We leave them in an enormous wooden tub and let them stand for a few weeks, till they get smelly.

Then comes the cooking part. First you dump the oolichans into another huge tub that has a fire on the ground under it. When it starts getting hot we let it cook for a certain number of hours, at a fixed temperature. While it cooks we have to keep stirring it or else it would all settle to the bottom and stick to the bottom of the tub. When the certain number of hours are up we have to take the clear yellow part out of the tub and put it into a big pail. We drain the thick part into the river.

When we make grease, we usually make it across the river from the village houses. Also when we make grease we usually make it just at the beginning of spring or around the end of April, or the first week in May.

One thing you have to be careful of is the smell of it. But it all depends on whether you like the grease when it is cooked or not. When you get home from making grease, you have to take a bath and change into clean fresh clothes.

To me, oh, grease tastes good! Mmm. Most of all our people

like oolichan grease. It doesn't taste like any other food or grease. It has its own delicious taste.

We have more than a dozen uses for oolichan grease. One is with boiled fish. When we boil it with fish we call it "usa". This is delicious in taste. Another way we use it is with seaweed. We boil the seaweed with a bit of water and pour some oolichan grease into the same pot that we used in which to boil the seaweed. This has the most delicious taste of all.

Another very important use is when we get sick we drink it. To us it is just like cough mixture. Sometimes we rub it on our back or chest to act as any other chest rub in curing a cold.

When we store grease we put the grease in gallon bottles and store it away from the sun. When the sun hits it, it tastes funny, so it's best to shelter it from the sun.

When the grease gets cold it turns a milky colour. But when it is just freshly cooked it is an orange, golden colour. When it is fresh does it ever look nice! But it tastes funny. When it's milky coloured it tastes good.

There is a superstition that I know about oolichans. It is, that after we've finished eating oolichans, we're not supposed to drink water. If we do it will flood.

CANOE PULLING

Rosemary Wilson

As winter passed and the sun came out and shone over the village, everyone came out and walked about to and fro.

One day Grandpa, accompanied by the little children, walked to the beach. They all helped to carry his tools down and wondered what he was going to do with them.

Just as we got to the beach, Jeff shouted out. "Grandpa, what's this long, long boat for?"

Grandpa said to him, "Son, come sit down and I'll tell you about this long, long canoe".

Many, many years ago my mother's father made this canoe and won many races against different villages. Every year we would come here to pull against each other. Sometimes twelve canoes would be out there. The men had to work hard. They had to get up at sunrise and run hard. If they didn't run they got sick fast because they had broken the laws of my mother's father, who was the one who asked his people to make his canoe, and to paddle with other men and to run to be strong.

Before going out to paddle the Father used to come to make the sign of the cross over them. After they came back the Father would give them blankets, dishes, wool, for the first canoe.

Each village gave something to the first canoe.

The old folks danced for them at the beach. All this would last a long time. They would play sticks around the fire. Then all would go home.

The time came again when we went to Cowichan for racing. The day was no good but we went. The water was angry. The wind made big waves, but my mother's father told us all to go out.

We lined up to go. My mother's father said we must stay up longest. In the first stretch of the race only five of the twelve canoes stayed up. Then we came back again. Only our canoe stayed up. All the others fell over. Not only did they fall over but the waves were so big and strong and the sea so deep, that many of the braves drowned.

We came back to the beach and the people shouted at us. They gave us blankets and sweaters. The Father gave us a silver cup.

This is why this long boat sits here today. People still come and want to buy it, but I say, "No", because it is a memory of my mother's father to his people. It saved all our lives.

OLDEN DAYS ABOUT INDIANS

Marion Peter

In the olden days Indians lived on fish such as dog-salmon, and whales, whenever the men got one. They also ate sea lions, fur seals and ducks, like geese and mallards. They also ate sea food like sea-urchin, Chinese shoes and mussels. They dried clams and sea lion meat and fish for the winter.

They used to put up feasts for the people in the Big House. While the women were preparing the meal the men would sing

Indian songs. They were fed deer meat, ducks or clams.

When making a fire they rubbed two dry cedar sticks together until there were sparks. They had the fire right in the middle of the house in the open and the house used to fill with smoke.

They made knives out of stone. They made harpoons for catching fish. Many Indians made fancy canoes, totem poles and masks. The women picked wild berries, such as blueberries, salmonberries, salal berries and many other kinds.

They had mostly wooden things, wooden dishes and wooden spoons.

On one occasion when the men were whale fishing they got one and it pulled them far out to sea until they found themselves in China!

THE LEGEND OF THE LOVERS

Pearl Wilson

There were once two young people who lived in a small village. The two were a beautiful young girl, and a brave. The maiden was called Morning-Glory and the brave was called White-Feather.

White-Feather fell in love with Morning-Glory, when he was quite young. When they were about sixteen years old the two were to be married by the Indian fashion, which usually never lasts.

As time went on Morning-Glory was growing impatient with White-Feather who didn't really like work. He would be at home waiting for Morning-Glory when she came home from work.

One day he had brought her to a place in Saanich to pick berries and there they weren't getting along too well. For about two years the young maiden wondered why she was putting up with White-Feather, not working all the time.

One day, when Morning-Glory was out washing their clothing, she found a handkerchief all wrapped up in the young brave's pocket. She opened it and found part of an animal's tail, and strands of her long hair, in a small bundle. This made Morning-Glory very curious, so in the later afternoon she took it to her parents, who knew many of the Indian ways.

Her mother told her of how a man used this animal's tail to keep the girl he was in love with. After Morning-Glory was through listening to her mother she began to wonder. When she got home she talked to White-Feather about the animal's tail and told him that she didn't realize how much he loved her. Soon White-Feather went hunting. He was happy to know that Morning-Glory knew he really loved her and he did all he could to please her.

THE TWO BROTHERS

Regina Charlie   Told by her father

This happened years ago in a place called Kyuquot, on the north end of Vancouver Island. The Chief from Kyuquot married a princess from Alert Bay. She moved to Kyuquot with her husband. They had two sons. In early times the older son in the family was brought up to have his younger brother serve him. The young brother was trained to go hunting and fishing with his father. He knew a great deal that his older brother did not know. He knew that the father of the boys was very strict. He beat the boys for burning him. The boys told the father that it was an accident. The father said it wasn't.

The boys went to their aunt, the sister of their father, and told her what had happened and said they were running away from home. She told them she would not tell anyone but she gave them advice. The boys made a plan. They put together a basket of dried fish and Indian tools. They went to bed early that night.

When everyone was asleep they knocked the night watchman out. There was always a night watchman to keep the fire going. The boys grabbed up their things and rushed off. They walked very far until they came to a lake. The older brother was worried about how to cross the lake, but the younger brother knew how. They crossed on a log raft. When they crossed the lake they stayed there overnight. In the morning they woke up early and made a fire. Again the older brother was worried. He knew that if anybody saw the smoke they would be discovered. But the younger knew how to prevent the smoke. He pulled some moss and put it over the flame. They ate and went on. They had to go over the Alberni Valley.

Finally they came to another Indian village called Alert Bay. They didn't allow themselves to be seen in the village. The first evening they got there they were peeking through a knot hole in the Chief's house. They didn't know it was their uncle, their mother's brother. The older boy fell in love with his own first cousin. He didn't know that they were cousins. One night the younger brother sneaked in while everybody was asleep. The princess bit his finger hard. He ran out of the house without a shout. He didn't make a sound because he knew the Chief would wake up and find him there. The two boys stayed in the woods for a week. They came back to the village when the younger boy's finger was healed.

The Princess told her father what had happened during the night. All the unmarried men were ordered to line up to have their fingers looked at. But none of them had a bitten finger. Later the Chief found out about the boys. He knew that one of the boys wanted his daughter for his wife. He arranged for tests between the two brothers. Because the older brother wanted to marry the princess, he and the girl had to sing an Indian song. The boy didn't know the song but his younger brother was hiding behind him and sang the song while his older brother was moving his lips.

Every day the younger brother was out hunting and fishing. The Chief didn't like the older boy and did not wish him to have his daughter, because he never went out hunting nor fishing.

In the end it was the younger brother who married the Princess. He was the chosen one because he had learned to do everything.

SPIRIT FINDERS

Edith Pelkey

One ceremony the Indians on the Saanich reserve have is, that when a person in the family dies, all the close relatives come and sit on a bench and put paint on their faces, so that the spirits will not enter into them. They get some bushes and light them, and go into all the rooms and chase the spirits out. They bring the fire all the way outside to make sure the spirits do not remain inside.

They brush this fire on the persons themselves to make sure the spirits do not go into another person. After this the people go out one by one, and an Indian woman has a basin of water and a special soap, and she washes your face and splashes the water out of the basin onto the ground to make sure that the spirits are dispersed. After this the mother or wife takes all the food and clothing out of the house and burns it. Between the time of the death and the burial, the wife or mother eats alone in a room and uses certain dishes and silverware. This goes on until after the burial.

This originated when a certain Indian woman's husband died and she was left by herself in their tent. Every day she went for a walk in the woods and she would see a hawk in a tree looking at her. Finally it began coming into her tent and making noises, but no one else could hear or see it. At last then she went to the Chief and told him that she continued to hear the bird in her tent. The Chief returned to the tent with her and the bird was still there. They began to throw fire about in the tent and as the fire burned, the spirit left. It did not come back to frighten the woman.

The Indians of today still practise these ceremonies after the death of one of their family.

AN INDIAN LEGEND

Roseanna Charlie

Of all the many interesting things which may seem strange to people other than the Indians are the customs surrounding death. The Indians have many customs and beliefs, but those concerning death are most sacred to them.

One custom is that when any of your relations die, you must feed and clothe the dead. It must be done at least once in the year. If you do not keep this custom, it shows that you do not have respect for your people. If you are not thinking of them or wanting to talk to them when they appear in your sleep, or when you are alone, something mysterious will happen to you.

First of all the person who is preparing to help their family will invite other members of the family to a feast.

The persons who are preparing the feast will carry the food that they have brought and prepared for the dead, and they will put it on platters. When this is ready the oldest or wisest Indian man will call the dead. Then they will pass the platters of food to him and say for whom it is intended. He will carry that person, and the platter of food is put on the logs with the fire under it. It is kept on the fire until they have passed all the food that they have prepared for their relatives.

Once the feast has started no one may leave because this would be an insult to the dead. Again trouble would come.

After a long while, when all the remaining food is burnt, the wisest Indian will tell the people all he has seen and what the old people have said.

Then the sorrowing begins. I have learned that if you cry and mourn for the late relative, you must rinse your face and hands before leaving the cemetery, or wherever you may be. If you do not then you will carry all the bitterness and sadness with you and this will make you ill. Perhaps you will die. So when the basin of water is passed around to the people all must wash before leaving.

A supper is then held and there is talk of all the people in the family. Everyone is thanked for coming to the supper and for attending the ceremonies of the dead. Money is given to all those who helped.

These ceremonies last all of one day and far into the night. They are different, but they are important to the Indian people who still observe them.

CRAFTS

A Mother's Promise

Rosemary Sabbas. Age 11. Grade 7
Hesquiaht Band
Christie Indian Residential School
Tofino. B.C.

Second Honourable Mention, 1964

Mask Making

Bertie Moon. Age 13. Grade 7
Tsawataineuk Band
Kingcome Inlet Indian Day School
Kingcome Inlet. B.C.

Nootka Basket Weaving

Lucy Andrews. Age 13. Grade 7
Hesquiaht Band
Christie Indian Residential School

The First Totem Carver

Judy Thomas. Age 16. Grade 8
Halalt Band
Kuper Island Residential School
Kuper Island. B.C.

A MOTHER'S PROMISE

Rosemary Sabbas   Told by her grandmother

There was once a tribe of Indians that had just settled in the dark Nootka forests. A member of the tribe was a young girl named Shaki. She was a very pensive girl because her mother, whom she had loved so much, had died. Shaki enjoyed roaming through the quiet forests, for there she could think about her mother and visit her grave.

One day she stood near the spot where her mother was buried. She noticed some thin green leaves growing there. They were so lovely, that Shaki picked them. Then, she came to a little stream that trickled happily over stones and moss. She sat there for a long time, and then she saw that the lovely thin leaves that she had picked had fallen into the stream. Quickly she picked them out and ran home with them. She wanted them to be a little gift for her father. As she stepped into the house, she noticed that her lovely leaves had become stiff and straight, yet they did not break.

At first, Shaki was sad, but then she decided that she would keep these lovely leaves, since she had found them beside her mother's grave. This she did.

That night, Shaki dreamed that her mother came to their home. She told Shaki to bring her the thin leaves. Shaki brought them, and when she handed them to her, her mother disappeared. The next morning Shaki awoke and remembered the dream. She looked for her lovely leaves, but they were gone. So, sadly she walked to her mother's grave to find more. How surprised she was when she reached the burial place! There on her mother's grave were her leaves. They were no longer just thin green leaves; they were woven into a beautiful little basket. Shaki's mother had not forgotten. This was the gift she had promised her before she had died. Shaki showed her basket to the Indian girls in the tribe, and she taught them how to make more. And to this day, the Indians of Nootka weave beautiful baskets.

MASK MAKING

Bertie Moon   Told by Peter Moon

My father carves masks to sell to people who buy them. He has made so many that I could not tell you just how many he has made. My favourite ones are the swan, the moon, the raven and the whale.

He learned how to make masks from his father. My dad was just a little boy when he was taught. From that time on my dad knew how to make masks.

My dad uses special tools to make a mask. His tools have to be sharp all the time, for if the tools are dull they will not cut well and will spoil the wood.

Some of the masks that my dad has made are animals and some look like human faces. There are some masks that my father has made that are just so colourful that I couldn't keep my eyes off them.

My dad said that they stand for what the Indian people used to believe in or things that are living today.

Carving masks is what my dad does for a living.

NOOTKA BASKET WEAVING

Lucy Andrews

My people, the Nootka Indians, have been weaving beautiful baskets for many generations, and the art of making these baskets has not changed in all these years.

Skilful Indians cut strips of grass which they call "Chitipt," and strips of bark from cedar trees. The Chitipt is washed in a basin and set out to dry in the warm sun. When the Chitipt is dry, it turns to a light brown colour, and is ready to be used. Some of this fine grass is placed in a pot of boiling dye, and then hung out to dry. This dyed grass is later used to weave designs such as eagles, whales and canoes, into the basket.

When the fine grass and the bark are ready, a wooden frame shaped like a basket is used to hold the weaving firmly in place. Then, shaping several pieces of dry bark around the wooden frame and placing a piece of sturdy cardboard on the bottom, the weaver begins at the bottom and weaves in and out, alternately in opposite directions.

Soon, the weaver is ready to make the designs with the dyed grass. These designs are usually copied from embroidered cloths which the Indian women make for this purpose. When the design is finished, the weaver continues the basket with plain dried grass. She then twines the bark which will be used for a handle, and sews it securely with more strips of dried grass.

Now the basket is complete, and this work of art travels to towns and cities, to keep alive the culture of my people.

THE FIRST TOTEM CARVER

Judy Thomas   Told by her grandfather

Many years ago before my grandfather's time there lived a young brave named Theomata. He lived by the river's edge in the land of sparkling waters.

Theomata spent his time alone while the tribesmen would hunt and fish, and while his mother with the rest of the women would work busily.

Often he would silently get into his canoe and cross the waters to the other side. There Theomata would cover his canoe carefully and wander off into the forest to a little clearing where stood a dead cedar tree.

Theomata would climb the tree, and with his axe he would cut, shape and chop the tree. He made fantastic shapes of his own design.

Beginning to carve from the top to the bottom, he carved an eagle with outstretched wings and ended with a toad. Other animals he made as he worked steadily on.

Sometimes he would work for hours until each curve and shape was perfect. In this way he worked to leave something of courage and adventure and hope for the generation to come.

Theomata brought a new art into existence though at that time he was not aware of it.

O Theomata if you hear me now listen to me carefully. Listen, O listen Theomata. Your great skill is going on. From generation to generation your craft of carving is being handed down. These great forms of yours are known as the Totem Poles.

Theomata, Theomata, these great poles have brought honour to our people. It is to you that we give our thanks. It is to you that we owe this means of livelihood. I know for my grandfather has lived mainly on his Totem Pole construction.

WARFARE

The Ambush that Failed

James Peter. Age 14. Grade 8
Kyuquot Band
Kyuquot Indian Day School
Kyuquot. B.C.

Trader George, the Great Indian Chief

Louise Martin. Age 11. Grade 6
Clayoquot Band
Opitsaht Indian Day School
Tofino. B.C.

THE AMBUSH THAT FAILED

James Peter   Told by his father

It was a cold night and the moon shone brightly. The sound of dancing feet and the beating of drums echoed over the still air of Markale.

Beside a Longhouse stood a cabin constructed of rough cedar boards. The cabin was inhabited by a middle-aged man. With his young friend for company, he was carving a mask.

Feeling thirsty he said, "Come we will get water." They walked out with their old wooden pail. Down the trail they went, talking happily about the celebration that was taking place in the village.

While stooping to draw water the man heard the cooing of a bird. Or was it a bird? It was a man! He could tell by the silhouette. He thought, "Every man is at the dance! This man has a bow and arrow in his hand. This means trouble."

The man wondered how he could take him without risk to himself or the villagers. "First I'll get rid of the pail," he thought. He filled the pail and took a drink. As he drank he had a better look at the invader.

"Should I warn my people or get the man first? " he asked himself. He took the pail home and on the way out he picked up his weapons. He circled around and came behind the man who was spying on the village.

He signalled him to come down. When he came, a club crashed into his skull and he stumbled to the ground. The victorious warrior carried him away. First he cut the head off the man and hid him under a log.

Into his cabin he then ran with his prize clutched in his hand. He set the head down and put his war dress on. Then to the celebrating house he ran.

To the announcer he said, "Tell them I have an especial dance, look!" He held the head level with his shoulder.

54

So he danced the war dance across the room several times. The people knew what had happened because they saw the man's war-painted face.

After the dance the men held their weapons and walked out one by one. The Chief halted them and said, "We will make sure that this raid will fail. Take a position of a 'V' from the north beach to this beach."

Then came the first two of the attackers, right into the hands of their enemies. Two by two they came. And two by two they were killed. Then no more came. The Chief said, "There are no more? Let us be sure."

On the way to the village they met two more raiders. They chased them, caught and killed them. "Now let us get their canoes," called the Chief.

In the moonlight the figures of three men could be seen guarding the canoes. Yelling, the warriors pursued them. The three men pushed out a canoe and paddled for life. "Let them go," cried the victorious villagers, as they walked home, some wounded but all of them happy.

TRADER GEORGE, THE GREAT INDIAN CHIEF

Louise Martin   Told by her grandparents

This story took place in the early days when Trader George of the Clayoquot tribe, whom the Indians called Shioush, invited the people from Nootka and Hesquiaht to attend a wedding. This was not a real wedding but a way in which to get the Indians from Nootka and Hesquiaht together, in order that Trader George might kill them.

First they had a big feast with dancing. When the dancing was under way, Trader George called all of his men inside the Big House and ordered them to get their weapons. There were about two hundred men from the two tribes who had been invited to the wedding feast at Clayoquot. Trader George had an equal number of men.

After receiving instructions the men of Clayoquot returned to the dancing grounds and while the dancing continued they waited for the signal from Trader George. Then they charged the

Chief of the Nootkas. A furious fight ensued with the men stabbing each other to death. Fifty of Trader George's men were left but none of the Nootkas and a few only from the Hesquiaht tribe.

When Sitakinim, or Trader Barney as he came to be called, saw the dead Nootkas hung up in the trees he was angered. Now it is said that Trader Barney was four feet wide and that his arms were very powerful. He could break steel or the bones of anyone. With only twenty of his tribe he set upon the remaining people of Clayoquot and subdued them. It was a long time before the people of Clayoquot were restored to a wealthy state again.

SEA CREATURES

The Legend of the Whale Hunters

Dominic Andrews. Age 14. Grade 7
Hesquiaht Band
Christie Indian Residential School
Tofino, B.C.

Third Prize, 1965

The Whaler

Lucy Gillette. Age 11. Grade 8
Kyuquot Band
Kyuquot Indian Day School
Kyuquot, B.C.

A Prayer Heard

Margaret Nicolaye. Age 14. Grade 6
Kyuquot Band
Kyuquot Indian Day School

First Prize, 1961

A Legend of the Spring Salmon

Joseph Ginger. Age 15. Grade 8
Uchucklisaht Band
Christie Indian Residential School

First Prize, 1963

The Indian Boy and the Herring

Agnes Oscar. Age 12. Grade 8
Kyuquot Band
Kyuquot Indian Day School

The Writings of Petroglyph Park

Verna Wpe, Age 12, Grade 7
Nanaimo Band
Quennell Provincial School
Nanaimo, B.C.

Smoked Salmon

Georgina Robinson, Age 10, Grade 4
Lakalzap Band
Indian Day School No. 800
Alert Bay, B.C.

The Boy Who Became a Sea Lion

James Peter, Age 15, Grade 8
Kyuquot Band
Kyuquot Indian Day School

First Prize, 1964

THE LEGEND OF THE WHALE HUNTERS

Dominic Andrews   Told by his grandmother

Among the Nootka whale hunters, long ago, there lived a brave, Ki-Yah, who was big and strong. Every day he would go out to hunt whales, with the other braves in the village.

One morning, as Ki-Yah prepared to set out for the hunt, he recalled the story that had been repeated so often by the wise, old men of his village. This tale told of a brave who would one day meet the king of the whales and who, upon their meeting, would receive one wish.

Soon, all was ready, and Ki-Yah and the other braves set out in their canoes. Ki-Yah's canoe moved swiftly across the water as the braves with him rowed steadily. Then suddenly a heavy mist surrounded them and the ocean grew very rough. Ki-Yah knew that whales were near, but he couldn't see anything. A sudden crash threw Ki-Yah out of the canoe. Although the other braves searched and searched, they could not find him. Sadly, they returned to their village. They did not know that Ki-Yah was, at this moment, having a strange adventure. For, after he had fallen out of the canoe, he had been picked up on the back of a whale and taken to the whale kingdom beneath the sea.

Now, Ki-Yah stood fearlessly before the throne of the whale king and listened to him speak. The whale king told Ki-Yah that he was the brave chosen to make any wish that he desired. The other whales listened, attentively, for Ki-Yah's words. They thought that he would ask for many riches and great power. But Ki-Yah knew in his heart what wish he would make. For although he never expected to be the chosen one, he had often thought about the wish, as the old men in his village repeated the tale.

Ki-Yah spoke, and when he had made his wish, all were silent. He had asked that his people might always live in peace with their neighbours.

Ki-Yah was truly a wise brave. for to this day. the Nootka Indians have lived in peace. And. as a reminder of Ki-Yah's friendship with the whales. the Nootka Indians still carve the image of the whale into their Totem Poles.

THE WHALER

Lucy Gillette   Told by her mother

Once there was a father who had three sons.

Early one morning the father was sitting outside when he saw a whale blow. He knocked on the side of the house to waken his sons and said to them, "There is a sperm whale close to the beach."

The sons got up and put their two canoes in the water and started after the whale. Soon the hunters harpooned the whale. The whale took them out to sea. The second canoe waved to the first because the men could not paddle fast enough to keep up. The strongest man jumped overboard from the first canoe and swam to the other canoe and started to paddle. He overtook the first canoe and lashed the two canoes together. The whale kept on going.

First they went through sandy water. So great was the exertion that the hunters were spitting blood over the bows of the canoe. Next they came to the choppy waters and the hunters did the same thing; spitting blood on both bows. When the whale finally stopped they were so far out that they could not see the land. The hunters did not go to sleep for four days and four nights.

Soon a little bird sat on the bow of one of the canoes and sang a little song and flew back to land. Then another bird flew to the bow of the other canoe and also sang a song. At the end of the song the whale started for the shore. with the men singing the same song all the way. The whale went up to every inlet until at last it was beached at the same place where it had first been sighted.

60

A PRAYER HEARD

Margaret Nicolaye

Not very long ago there lived an old woman who was very poor and had no close friends at all.

She used to go around every day to every house trying to get her meal from the other people.

One day this little old woman couldn't find a place to eat and nobody seemed to want her any more.

She was disappointed and she was angry too. She made up her mind to move away from the people. She moved away to the other side of the village. She took everything she had and moved into a small cave.

Living in a cave she was not very happy. She used to go down to the beach to gather up driftwood for her fire. Every day when the tide was low she used to go down to dig for clams and mussels.

It was hard for her when the weather was bad. She couldn't get most of the sea foods that she was used to living on. She spent most of the day singing and praying that she might find some better food to eat and a better place to live in.

One day, after a big storm was over, she woke up early and went down to the beach as usual. She walked a little way across the beach hoping to find something.

At the end of the beach she found a small fish, a rock cod. She was happy to find it, but not quite satisfied with it. She would rather find something bigger. She thought she would leave this little fish while praying for a bigger one. She didn't pick it up. She tied the little fish with a line and left it at the same place. She stayed up praying all night, and between prayers she sang some old songs. She was praying for a bigger fish.

Early in the morning, at daybreak, she went down to see the little fish. She was still praying, and making herself believe that this small fish was a whale. She pulled on the line and dragged the fish up a little way. Then she went back to her cave and went to sleep. She slept all day. In the evening she woke up and started praying again, for a bigger fish. She did the same thing for four nights and every morning she pulled up the fish a little way. A storm came up again which lasted a few days more.

At the end of the storm it was also her last night of prayer. When the morning came she put her blanket on and went down to the beach to look around. She hadn't gone very far when to her surprise she saw with her own eyes a big dead whale which had drifted ashore on her beach that stormy night.

At first she didn't know what do do. She knew that her prayers were heard. She started singing her songs and she built a big fire on the beach and all the people were wondering what was going on. The couple who had hated her the most were the first to come to find out. They were very much surprised to see the big fish.

All the people came down to the beach where the big fish was cut up. All the Kyuquot tribe had a good share of the whale. And the little woman was looked after by every member of the tribe from that day on.

A LEGEND OF THE SPRING SALMON

Joseph Ginger   Told by his mother

Once in spring, many moons ago, a young Indian brave, having compassion on a starving slave gave him some dried fish to eat. His mother, angered by her son's pity for a lowly slave, chided him severely.

Grieved by his mother's attitude, the brave left his village in a war canoe and paddled aimlessly along the river until he found himself at the shoreline of a strange village, where the carvings on the Longhouse indicated that the inhabitants belonged to the Spring Salmon Tribe.

The brave was welcomed warmly by the Spring Salmon Chief, who explained to the brave that because of his kindness to the slave, his health had been restored to him, for the slave in reality, was a member of the Spring Salmon Tribe.

Then the Spring Salmon Chief expressed his gratitude in a strange way. He offered the young brave hospitality and instructed him to club one of the children playing outside the Longhouse whenever he was hungry. When the brave expressed horror at such an idea, the Chief explained that this would not harm the child, it would only cause it to be turned into a spring salmon. However, he was cautioned by the Chief to be sure to burn the eyes and the bones of each fish after he had eaten. For, in this way, the fish would again return to their land, if it was burned within the season.

The brave followed the Chief's directions but once, when he carelessly neglected to burn the eye of a salmon of which he had eaten, a child in the village complained of a sore eye. As soon as he burned the eye the child's ailment disappeared.

And thus it was that from then on, every time the members of the Spring Salmon Tribe had feasted on their fish, they immediately burned the eyes and the bones, and every spring the salmon returned to their waters.

Because salmon was the main sustenance of many Indian tribes in the past, it was respected and even worshipped as a God. That respect remains, in part, even to this day.

THE INDIAN BOY AND THE HERRING

Agnes Oscar

Once upon a time there was a very poor family. In this family there were four sisters and three brothers.

Their parents used to sell or smoke herring for a living but there was often so little that the youngest in the family was only allowed to smell the food.

One day when this little boy was alone, a spirit spoke to him and told him to eat all the food that he could find. After about an hour of persuasion the boy did as he had been told.

In the early afternoon when his mother came and found that he had eaten all the food she punished him. Every day she punished him when she found that he continued to eat all the food.

On a certain day the boy went to the beach. When he got there he couldn't believe what he saw. Suddenly great numbers of herring appeared in the water, so many that the sea seemed to be thick with them.

The boy ran to tell his father and older brothers.

The little boy's father sold the herring and his mother smoked many for winter use.

That night the Indian boy said a prayer of thanksgiving for sending the herring.

The boy's mother never punished him again and they all lived happily ever after.

THE WRITINGS OF PETROGLYPH PARK

Verna Wpe   Told by her father

At the time of this story all of the Indians had their own beliefs.

At this time there were no fish coming up the Nanaimo River except rock cod. So the mink, beaver and muskrat settled around a council fire. The animals tried to figure out a way to bring the salmon up the Nanaimo River. They decided to go to visit the Salmon people in the north. They made plans with the woodpecker and kingfisher to help capture the baby sockeye salmon.

When they got there the kingfisher and woodpecker started a fish to distract the Salmon people from their work, and they gathered around them. As the Salmon people talked with the beaver, the mink and the muskrat stole the baby sockeye.

After they discovered the baby missing the Salmon people gave chase up the Nanaimo River.

Mink and muskrat moved the baby from place to place and made markings wherever they took the baby. They made markings at Malaspina Point, Jack's Point and Petroglyph Park.

And from that time on, every year the salmon come up the Nanaimo River, looking for the baby salmon.

SMOKED SALMON

Georgina Robinson   Observed by her aunt

First of all my uncle mends his net, then he borrows a wheelbarrow to carry his net to the beach. He has somebody help put it in his boat. He gives the wheelbarrow back to the owner. Then he starts off to wet his net. He picks a part where the water is so deep you can't see the bottom. Then he sets the net there. Then he makes sure it is properly set, so the fish won't get out. He leaves the net for two or three days. He goes back out to see his net. Then he pulls it up and takes the fish out and brings them home. My aunt comes out to meet him. She helps him bring them in.

She gets the fish ready for the smoke-house. She takes a salmon and cuts its head off, but leaves the tail on. Then she cuts

64

it open along the line that is on it. She starts to cut in at the vent. Then she takes the liver out. She cuts the blood vein open and takes the blood out. To flatten it she cuts two or three slices from each side of the fish. To get the bones out, she cuts under the bones with the tail joined to them. She throws the head and tail with the bones joined to it, into a can nearby. When this is all done, she hangs it on a kind of thin wood in a house which is called a smoke-house. There is a hot fire under the wood, on which the fish is hanging. But the fire must not touch the fish or it will burn. It must hang one or two yards high. It does not matter if the flame dies, but the smoke has to rise. We boil it or bake it over a hot stove. With potatoes the fish makes a delicious dinner. Now my mouth is watering to have some. Is yours?

THE BOY WHO BECAME A SEA LION

James Peter   Told by his father

There lived a boy. He was the only boy in his family. This boy was very lazy. All he did was lie in bed all day. If a beautiful day dawned he would go out on the porch and do nothing all day. He was so lazy that even his body was unkempt. His legs and neck were very dirty.

So his father could stand it no more and he was angry. "My son, you should not sleep so much. You should do something. The other boys in the village who are your age are out shooting ducks." On saying this the angry father picked up a stick and beat his son.

After this the boy started bathing. Every night, when everyone was sleeping, he went bathing in a river on the other side of the village. He went bathing every night for one week. Before day came, he went into the house and rubbed dirt off the earth floor onto his body, so that his plans should not be known.

During one of his walks along the beach to his bathing place he found a sleeping sea lion. He killed the great animal and skinned it. Then he hid the body of this sea lion. He cleaned the big sea lion skin so that he could use it.

Another night came. The boy went to where the sea lion was hidden in the woods. With the great skin on, he began diving. At first he dived a short way. The boy did not give up. Gradually he went further and further. He thought he was not going deep enough, so off the beach he took up a smooth, round pebble, as large as an egg. With this in his hands he could stay under longer.

After many nights he could dive far down, coming up for air once in a while. He did not reveal himself and he travelled in the darkness of night and all day, along the coast towards the north.

Here and there he found many sea lions resting and sleeping. This boy in the sea lion skin dived and dived. When he was tired he stopped with the sea lions, who were always on the rocks resting. He would climb up on the rocks in the fashion of the great sea creatures, but they would scatter from him in fright.

Swimming up the coast of Vancouver Island, he reached Cape Scott. Then a strange thing happened to the boy. He ate the raw foods of the sea lions and he became altogether like the creatures. He dived with ease and went great distances.

Then the brave boy did the most daring thing. He left the land and went to the open sea towards the Queen Charlotte Islands.

Many days and nights the boy in the sea lion skin travelled. Finally he saw land after many weeks of diving and swimming.

He was not only interested in the land. He looked for the sea lions swimming or resting on the rocks. In time he sighted sea lions on a rocky little island. He approached it in the sea lion's fashion and climbed up the rocks. When he was among the sea lions everything changed. The sea lions were no longer sea creatures but living people like himself. The rocks were no longer there and a great house took their place.

After all his travelling a Spirit had entered him and he was the sea lion, but he thought himself to be unchanged and just a boy in a sea lion skin.

Among the sea lion people he observed the men who had been fish hunting entering their homes with nothing but rock cod and black bass. These fish, the boy knew, were not living in deep water.

To the Chief of the sea lion people, with whom he was living, he said, "I also am going fishing".

To the deep water he dived and caught many halibut. He came to his home and the people were very impressed that a sea lion should get a deep water fish. They asked him how he could dive so deep. They said they could dive only in the shallows. He refused to tell them and kept his secret that he was a human.

The Chief of the sea lions was very proud of the boy and he

made him marry his daughter. This woman was a sea lion. A while after, they had two sons, and they were little sea lions.

Here the boy in the sea lion skin stayed. Every once in a while he would go fish hunting. He would get halibut, salmon, and even hair seals. The sea lions became very wealthy in food because of the young fellow.

But when he was hunting one day he saw a village. He wished he were there and walking on solid ground. But he stayed in the water swimming back and forth, waiting for nightfall. Then came the night and he went ashore. He did not go to the village beach. He went a distance from the village and walked the rest of the way. At the village he knew where the Chief's house might be. He approached the Chief's house, which was very large. Between the planks he peeked into the house and saw a girl. He went into the house and pushed the girl.

The girl just asked, "Who are you?" The boy refused to tell. He just started a conversation. Before daybreak he left and said, "I will be back. I want to be married with you. Ask your parents if I may have your hand in marriage."

He went back to his sea lion skin and put it back on. Back into the sea he went. He stayed there all day waiting for night to come. Late at night he came back to the girl. She told him he was to stay there—that they were going to be married.

He woke in the morning to hear that there was a great sea lion on the beach sleeping. To his wife he said, "That sea lion is what I have come in. My home is a great distance away."

Here he lived with the unknown people. He had left the sea lion people to be with a new wife. He lived there for many years hunting and fishing for the people. The girl's father liked him very much because he always came back from hunting with a lot of food for everyone.

After many years with the people, two sons were born to him. Then a thought struck him. He was wondering if his parents were all right. At that time the boy had a sea-gull. Every time the gull came in from flying somewhere he would tell his master what he had seen and where he had been.

The boy took his sea-gull and said, "I want you, my pet, to fly far to the south where my parents live. I ran away from them a long time ago because my father used to scold me and beat me."

He told the sea-gull that the great house might be all disassembled, with only the framework standing. He told the sea-gull how the village was and where it was. The boy understood the sea-gull's language and the sea-gull could understand him.

Then the sea-gull flew and flew to the south. He reached the village and found the place the boy had described. He landed on the rafter of the great framework and listened to the woman crying and talking about her lost son. On seeing this the sea-gull flew home back to his master. When he reached the village he told the boy how his parents felt. Hearing this the boy almost wept. Again the boy made his trusty pet fly to his parents. This time he put his ear-rings on the sea-gull. These ear-rings showed that he was a chief. The little sea-gull flew through the air with a pair of ear-rings on.

Towards the parents home the sea-gull flew. Many days he flew towards the destination. He arrived there. He looked for the old woman who always sat on the beach. If she were not there on the beach, the boy had told him to enter the hut.

Into the little house walked the sea-gull. He went to meet the old man, but he was kicked by the rude man. He was discouraged and he flew onto the woman's lap. She started petting him, for she was kind. She smiled and talked to the sea-gull. The sea-gull turned its head and she saw the ear-rings.

Excitedly she said to her husband, "Come quickly! Come and see! Look! This must be our son!"

At this they wept. The old man who had kicked the sea-gull picked it up and held it in his arms. At that moment they were beginning to eat. They began eating and they had their sea-gull in between them, for they thought it was their lost son.

There came a visitor who was called over by the man to see the ear-rings on the sea-gull. The man said, "Go you to get my crier. Tell him I want him."

The visitor rushed over to the crier and told the man he was wanted on an important matter. The crier went to the Chief and he was told to tell the people his son was back.

The sea-gull remembered that his master had said, "Do anything my parents want you to do."

That same day the great house was rebuilt and that night there was a great feast to honour the sea-gull. But the following morning the sea-gull disappeared. He was flying back to his master. He arrived and went straight to his master.

The little pet walked back and forth in front of the boy and told him how the parents were. The boy laughed at the thought of the sea-gull being dressed in a festival costume.

The boy decided to go home and he told the people of the village where he was living. They got ready to go and they set out in the four large canoes. The boy said, "It is not I who will guide you. My pet sea-gull will fly ahead and land just in sight of us. When we reach him he will again take off, and fly towards the direction of my home."

Then they began their journey, following the sea-gull. Many weeks they travelled until the boy said the land was becoming familiar.

The canoes turned shorewards. When they were in sight of a village the boy was struck dumb. He couldn't speak. When they hit the beach the people from the canoes immediately went up the shore, and the parents who had lost their son saw him, not as a boy, but as a grown man. He had four sons: the two boys with him and his present wife, and the sea lions by his sea lion wife, whom he had met when he was in the sea lion skin.

LAND ANIMALS

The Beaver

Laura Goldsmith. Age 11. Grade 3
Cowichan Band
St. Catherine's School
Duncan. B.C.

Second Honourable Mention, 1966

The Challenge

Mary Anne Charleson. Age 12. Grade 6
Hesquiaht Band
Christie Indian Residential School
Tofino. B.C.

A Bear Attacks the Berry Pickers

Betty Nicolaye. Age 14. Grade 7
Kyuquot Band
Kyuquot Indian Day School
Kyuquot. B.C.

A Strange Journey

Annabelle Brown. Age 14. Grade 7
Kyuquot Band
Christie Indian Residential School

The Boy Who Turned into a Dog

Norah Short. Age 13. Grade 7
Kyuquot Band
Kyuquot Indian Day School

Sta-Ka-Ya and the Wolves

Yvonne Sam. Age 13. Grade 7
Tsartlip Band
Brentwood School
Brentwood Bay. B.C.

The Wolf That Kept His Promise

Pamela Dawson. Age 11. Grade 5
Tsawataineuk Band
Kingcome Inlet Indian Day School
Kingcome Inlet. B.C.

First Prize, 1966

The Wolves

Beverley Charlie. Age 15. Grade 8
Cowichan Band
Kuper Island Residential School
Kuper Island. B.C.

Second Honourable Mention, 1963

Deer

Richard Thomas. Age 15. Grade 8
Halalt Band
Kuper Island Residential School

The Cougar, or The First Mosquitoes

Marilyn Marshall. Age 11. Grade 6
Ahousaht Band
Christie Indian Residential School

The Origin of the Snake

Edith Pelkey. Age 14. Grade 8
Tsawout Band
Kuper Island Residential School

The Legend of Snake Island

David Sylvester, Age 14, Grade 5
Penelakut Band
Kuper Island Residential School

Third Prize, 1966

Legend of Six Frogs

Joan Morris, Age 14, Grade 7
Songhees Band
Kuper Island Residential School

First Prize, 1962

THE BEAVER

Laura Goldsmith   Told by her father

This is a true story. The beaver is like a human being. He usually stays in the water. One day the beaver lost his carved stick. Then the beaver went to the Chief in the village. When the beaver went in, the Chief asked what he wanted. The beaver said, "I have lost my carved stick." The Chief said, "I have one here but I don't think it is yours." Then the beaver went into the water. He made a tunnel to go to all the houses. So one day the beaver went back to the Chief to ask for the stick. The beaver knew that the stick was his. Then the Chief laughed at the beaver. He said, "Get this man out of here." Then the beaver said, "I am not going until I get my stick." The Chief was laughing at the beaver's tail. The beaver got mad and took the stick. After he took the stick he stamped his tail on the floor. When he stamped his tail the whole village shook like thunder. Then all the houses fell into the holes that the beaver had made. The beaver laughed and said, "This will be the end of this village." The only one that was left in the village was the brave beaver.

THE CHALLENGE

Mary Anne Charleson   Told by her grandmother

Cautiously, Kon-Ka crept through the dismal forest, for he had been challenged by his enemy Monikaka. The one to emerge first from this forest would be the chief.

Now, everyone knew that no one had ever travelled through this forest and come out alive, for it was said to be filled with evil spirits. But Kon-Ka was a good brave, and though he was fearful, he went steadily on.

As he was nearing the edge of the forest, he heard a sudden cracking of a twig. Kon-Ka turned quickly, and there stood a large bear. He grabbed his knife and was about to stab it, when the bear shouted that she was in need of help. Kon-Ka feared that this might be a trick, but his kind heart could not refuse the bear, so he followed it to a cave. Here he found the bear's cub dying of fever. Kon-Ka set to work at once. For a whole day he nursed the dying cub until, at last, the fever began to leave him. Kon-Ka remained in the cave until the cub was completely cured. The bear was very grateful, and she and Kon-Ka became good friends. As they were about to part, the bear noticed the sad look in Kon-Ka's eyes and asked him what was the matter. Kon-Ka told the bear of his challenge with Monikaka and how he would surely lose the race now. The bear told Kon-Ka to follow her, for she knew a short cut through the forest. She led him safely through, and as Kon-Ka emerged from the forest, his people began the chant of victory. Kon-Ka's kindness was rewarded, and he had won. As for Monikaka, he was never seen or heard from again.

A BEAR ATTACKS THE BERRY PICKERS

Betty Nicolaye   Told by her father

One fine morning an old woman asked one of the younger women to go up the inlet to pick berries. They took some lunch and started off. The old woman and the girl paddled happily all the way for it was a beautiful morning.

Upon arriving at the place they were heading for, they tied up the canoe and picked up their baskets and went into the woods. They hadn't gone far when they came to a little swamp where they were to pick the berries. There was grass in the middle of this area and tall trees all around.

The two women started picking the berries. The berries were nice and ripe. The old woman was so busy picking that she forgot all about her companion and went quite a way from the young girl.

All at once the young girl called to the old woman to run down to the canoe as fast as she could, for there was a big black bear attacking her. She told the old woman to hurry home and to tell her friends to come and pick her up. While the girl was running the bear was very close behind her. She told the old woman to go quickly. The bear was jumping at her and tore a piece of her clothing and scratched her with its sharp claws on her legs and cut her skin right down to the bone.

She did not run for long around the open space. for she had scratches on her back too and she was losing her strength. Though she would not give up. she fell to the ground. She looked back and found that the bear was down too. right close to her and with his tongue hanging out, and breathing fast. Before the bear could jump at her again she started running again around the same grassy space, but not for long as she was by now very weak. She fell again. The bear was down too. The girl knew that she was getting very weak now because she had lost a lot of blood and there was pain in her body and legs.

Every time the bear jumped at her. she would turn around and put her basket on the bear's face. By doing this the bear would slow down because he had to fight the basket. The girl in this way gained a few steps.

The last time she fell she didn't lie long. She crawled on her knees to a stump nearby and climbed up on top of it. She knelt on the stump and started to pray loudly, and looking up at the sky. The bear also looked up to the sky. Then he looked down and seemed to become ashamed of what he had done to the young girl.

Now the old woman had seen everything that was going on as while she was hiding she was watching all the time. She then ran from her hiding place and went to the canoe. and taking it she paddled as fast as she could for home.

Arriving at the village she hollered for help, telling the people that the girl was dead and that she had been attacked by a big bear.

At the village a group of young men got together with their weapons and taking a canoe they went to help the girl.

The young woman continued to pray loudly. The bear got up and went off into the woods.

The girl then got down from the stump and lay down. for she was very weak from her wounds. It had been noon when the bear first attacked her. Now it was sun-down.

The young men arrived in the big canoe. They went to look for the bear and the girl, but they could not find the bear. They found the girl lying on the grass, weak and ill. They wrapped the girl up with a blanket. and put up a small tent. There they left her and told her that they would be back to pick her up on the fourth day.

The girl slept that night in her tent. In her sleep she saw the bear. The bear told her that he was sorry for what he had done to her and he said that he would make her well again.

So the bear licked the girl's wounds that night. Every night for four nights in her dreams the bear came and licked her wounds.

At the end of four days the young men came back to fetch the young woman and found that she was well and strong again.

A STRANGE JOURNEY

Annabelle Brown   Told by her mother

Once many many years ago, there lived in the village of A-oaks. a brave Indian, Kla-kish-pak. Every morning Kla-kish-pak used to walk through the forest until he came to a wishing pool, and there he would bathe.

On one of these mornings, as Kla-kish-pak bathed, a wolf sat at a distance and watched him. For three successive mornings the wolf watched, and each day he sat a little closer to the pool. On the fourth day, the wolf leaped out and took hold of Kla-kish-pak telling him to jump on his back. Kla-kish-pak was frightened, but he obeyed, and as he climbed on the wolf's back, he was told that they were going to journey to the wolf land. Kla-kish-pak was warned not to speak nor to open his eyes.

Far, far away they journeyed, and at last they came to the land of wolves. There, Kla-kish-pak was treated as though he were a wolf. He was made to hunt for hair seals and sea lions, and he was trained to be brave and strong. For four years, Kla-kish-pak lived with the wolves, and he learned well. Then, one day, all the wolves gathered together and their leader spoke to Kla-kish-pak and told him that he was now ready to return to his people and to become their leader. Two hundred wolves accompanied him on his journey home, and when they arrived at A-oaks the wolves were saddened by the thought of having to leave Kla-kish-pak, for they had grown to love him. As Kla-kish-pak bade farewell to his animal friends, they began to howl mournfully. And to this day, the plaintive cries of the wolves for Kla-kish-pak, are still heard.

THE BOY WHO TURNED INTO A DOG

Norah Short   Told by her grandfather

Once there was a boy who was always ill-treating his dog. Every time he saw it he would strike it with a stick or kick it. This continued for a long time.

Finally the dog grew tired of this treatment. He gathered the other dogs in a group and told them he was going to have a meeting. At the meeting they decided that the boy should be punished. The boy's punishment would be that he would be turned into a dog.

After the boy was turned into a dog, he and all the other dogs used to run down to the beach, take off their skins and bathe in the water. This occurred at night and it happened many times.

One night a man saw the dogs take off their skins and jump into the water. He went the next night to watch this strange occurrence again. When the boy took off his dog skin he would become a boy again but at the same time he would imitate the other dogs. The next time the man saw this happen he ran and grabbed the skin of the dog. When the boy returned to put the skin back on he found that it was missing.

When the other dogs were not looking the man grabbed the boy and brought him to his parents.

For some time after that, the boy ate garbage about the village, but soon after he became quite normal again.

STA-KA-YA AND THE WOLVES

Yvonne Sam   Told by her father

A long, long time ago there was a little Indian boy who liked to wander in the forest. While wandering he came upon six wolf cubs. He looked around for the mother of these cubs, but she was nowhere to be found. So every day he would go into the forest and feed the six cubs. He often would day-dream that one day he would be a great hunter, like his father. Finally, he thought to himself, "I will take the name of the wolf, which is Sta-Ka-Ya." As the years rolled by he grew up to be a husky brave.

Finally his father said, "Well, my son, it is time for you to go out and prove to us that you are going to be a great and brave hunter."

So Sta-Ka-Ya set out to prove himself. This was in the middle of the winter. As he climbed the mountain to hunt for deer it suddenly started to snow. He got his two deer, but the problem was to bring them down the mountain and back to camp. But before he started down a blizzard came. He tried to look for shelter and was fortunate to find an old log into which he was able to crawl and to cover himself. In this way he kept warm through the night.

When he woke in the morning the blizzard had stopped. He looked out and there were six huge wolves circling the old rotten log which Sta-Ka-Ya had taken refuge in. He thought of the six cubs that he had cared for. As he stepped out he saw the six wolves carrying his two huge bucks down the mountain side for him.

From then on, whenever he went hunting, these same wolves would be there to carry his bucks for him. They were always his companions while hunting. Twice his life was at stake, but always the six wolves were present to lead him back to camp in safety.

And so Sta-Kay-Ya became a legend for his great exploits as a hunter.

THE WOLF THAT KEPT HIS PROMISE

Pamela Dawson

Once there were some Indians in the Skeena River district who were getting hungrier and hungrier each day.

One morning the Chief found a wolf outside his tent. He asked it what it was doing there, but it didn't answer. So the Chief got some fish that was left over, and gave it to the wolf. But the wolf would not eat it. The Chief was wondering what was the matter with it. So he called his best medicine men and told them to make a quick search over the wolf. When the wolf knew what they were doing, it opened its mouth. So the Indians looked inside. They were surprised to see a big bone stuck in the wolf's throat. They took the bone out. Then the wolf gulped down the food that the Chief had given him.

When the wolf finished the fish, he said, "Thank you," with tears in his eyes. "Some day I will help your tribe."

One day in the winter the tribe had nothing to eat. The men were all thin, and the women complained that they were too cold to work. All the youngsters cried because they could not understand that there was no food.

Then they heard someone say, "If you want food, follow me." The Indian Chief knew right away that this was the voice of the wolf that they had saved. The men were afraid to follow the wolf, so they said, "He wants us to go with him so that he can kill us, then eat us." So the Indian Chief said that he and his brother would go.

The wolf had waited quite a long time. When the Chief saw that the wolf had killed some deer for him and his tribe he called out, "The wolf has helped us." Then he flung himself on one of the deer, ripped off a huge chunk and started eating hungrily.

When the wolf knew they had had enough he said, "I did this because you helped me when I came to you." Then he walked off towards the woods saying, "Everybody has got to help somebody."

THE WOLVES

Beverley Charlie   Told by her grandmother

One night our grandmother told us a story. It went like this.

The wolves lived long ago. It was believed that Indian people were turned into wolves by a witch doctor. This witch doctor was very jealous of his Indian people and put a curse on them by making them wolves. Once when the people were hunting they met the wolves. They were going to kill these wolves because the wolves used to steal their food, such as fish and deer meat.

Just as they were about to kill the wolves they heard the wolves speak in Indian to them. The wolves said that they would bring more fish and deer meat to them. The people were very frightened and wondered how the wolves had learned to talk in the Indian language.

One day a brave was fishing and a wolf came up to him and asked for some fish. The wolf said if he gave him some fish he would tell him how he became a wolf, but he was to tell no one.

So the Indian brave gave him some fish and the wolf told him what had happened. The witch doctor had put a curse on the people whom he disliked and the wolf said that he was one of those on whom the curse had been put. The Indian brave asked where the rest of the tribe was. In reply the wolf answered that some were dead and that others were wandering in search of food.

"Is there no hope for them?" asked the Indian brave.

"There is hope, but it is hard to find them in a place that is so big," the wolf replied.

The Indian brave asked what he could do. The answer was to kill the witch doctor. So the Indian braves gathered together and went in search of the witch doctor. They killed him, which set the wolves free.

Everyone rejoiced that the curse was lifted. After this the Indians no longer existed as wolves. They lived happily as Indian people as they do to this day.

DEER

Richard Thomas

A long time ago there was a Halalt runner who was more swift than any of the other braves. He was so fast that his parents named him "Swift Deer" which in the Indian language means a swift runner. In all the races this young man won the prize.

One day the son of the witch doctor entered the race. Swift Deer beat him by many yards. The witch doctor was angry and he made horns to grow on the head of Swift Deer and he gave him four legs instead of two, and Swift Deer could no longer think as he used to. But he could hear more acutely and he could run faster than ever. The witch doctor had turned him into a new animal.

Then one day he was aware of the hunters coming and Swift Deer ran as fast as he could, but one of the hunters shot and killed Swift Deer.

When the men got back to the village they talked of the great speed of this animal that they had shot. They said that it ran as fast as Swift Deer himself. Since they had not seen Swift Deer for a long time and did not know where he was they named this animal after him.

To this day the deer remain on Vancouver Island, keen of hearing and fleet of foot.

THE COUGAR or THE FIRST MOSQUITOES

Marilyn Marshall   Told by her aunt

Once upon a time an Indian brave made his way through the forest. As he crept silently through the trees and bushes a sudden cracking of twigs and the heavy panting of an animal alerted him. The brave crouched motionless and waited. Secretly he hoped it would be the vicious cougar that had challenged and killed many of the Indian braves and feasted on their blood. Was he to meet this same beast and suffer a similar fate?

As these thoughts flashed through his mind the sleek, tawny body of the cougar approached menacingly. The brave steadied his bow and arrow and shot. The arrow hit but it did not kill. Enraged by the stinging wound the cougar pounced on the brave, who waited for him with his knife in his hand.

The brave fought desperately and at last he had the beast down. With all his strength he plunged the knife deep into the cougar's body. The blood of all the animal's victims gushed out.

The brave quickly built a fire and burned the body of the cougar, as he had been instructed by his chief to do.

As the last ember died out the wind scattered the ashes of this blood-thirsty beast. As they rose into the air the ashes became mosquitoes. That is why the mosquitoes suck blood to this very day.

THE ORIGIN OF THE SNAKE

Edith Pelkey   Told by an elder

Long, long ago there was a man named Hissing Man. He was named this because whenever he went to the dances of the Indians he always made fun of them. He didn't believe in the dances, so he ridiculed them by hissing. He did this for quite a while. Then the chief of the tribe was so disgusted that he put this man out of the tribe. The man wandered around to the other tribes doing the same thing. Each tribe he went to, he was eventually put out.

The spirits were very displeased with him because they had given him many chances and he didn't take any of them. They became so displeased that one day they took away his arms and legs without him knowing. His voice was also taken from him, and all that was left was the hissing sound, but this he didn't want any more.

So from then on he had to crawl around on the ground without any legs and arms and make that strange hissing sound. This was the day that the snake was put on earth.

All the descendants and relatives of Hissing Man are condemned to roam the world in this same manner because of the terrible mistake made by Hissing Man.

THE LEGEND OF SNAKE ISLAND

David Sylvester

Along the road to our village there is an ordinary plant but it can tell a strange tale. It is about two feet tall. It has no leaves but the stem is almost like the head of a snake.

A young Indian had often seen the old people pick these plants, boil them and eat them. He did as they did. But when he ate he became very sick. At times he would get very dizzy and hungry. He would eat, but this would do no good because some strange creatures seemed to be crawling around inside of him and eating his food.

He told his grandmother that he could never eat enough. He was always hungry. One of the old Indians told his grandmother that he must have snakes in his body.

He said that they would take the young boy to a certain island where there was a lot of fruit. If he ate these fruits for two days he would be cured.

They took him to a little island not too far from Kuper Island, where they left him for two or three days. When they returned they found him lying face down in the grass. As they turned him over many snakes dropped from his body. He was weak but still alive. The men carried him hurriedly to the boat. The snakes seemed to be following them, even into the water, as they climbed into the little row boat.

To this day many snakes are still to be found on Snake Island.

LEGEND OF SIX FROGS

Joan Morris   Told by her grandmother

Once upon a time there lived a family at the West Saanich Reserve, near a pond. There were seven children in this family, from the ages of seven to fourteen years.

One day they all decided to go hunting together, so they asked permission of their parents.

Just as they were leaving the father took them aside and told them if they stopped at the pond to eat their lunch, they were not to eat anything that they found there. After this they bade farewell to their father and set out in their canoe.

As they were approaching the pond one of them asked if they should stop and eat, as he was very hungry. So they all stopped and ate some of their lunch.

As they were eating one of them noticed a piece of paper with something wrapped inside it. So they all went to see what it was.

When one of the bigger boys opened it they found all sorts of food and dry fish. It looked so delicious that six of the boys started eating, but one of them remembered what his father had told them and he tried to stop his brothers. But they laughed at him and said that he was superstitious, like their father.

Not long after they all felt strange. Then looking at one another they noticed that each one was getting smaller and smaller. Gradually all six of them changed into little green frogs.

The one that did not change got in the canoe and paddled home to tell his father what had happened.

After supper the father told the mother the sad news. Suddenly they heard the croaking of frogs outside and going out they noticed the six little frogs. These little frogs stayed there until winter.

That is how the frogs came to the West Saanich Reserve.

BIRDS

An Unfinished Journey

Bruce McCarthy. Age 15. Grade 8
Uchucklisaht Band
Christie Indian Residential School
Tofino, B.C.

First Honourable Mention, 1964

The Spirit of the Owl

David Henry. Age 18. Grade 8
Cowichan Band
Kuper Island Residential School
Kuper Island, B.C.

Owls

Willard Pelkey, Age 15, Grade 8
Cowichan Band
Kuper Island Residential School

A Lesson Too Late

James Short, Age 15, Grade 8
Kyuquot Band
Christie Indian Residential School

Second Honourable Mention, 1966

The Owl

Floyd Edwards, Age 17, Grade 8
Penelakut Band
Kuper Island Residential School

The Black Birds

Richard Thomas. Age 15. Grade 8
Halalt Band
Kuper Island Residential School

The Greedy Old Raven

Peter Hanson. Age 11. Grade 5
Kyuquot Band
Kyuquot Indian Day School
Kyuquot, B.C.

Third Prize, 1961

Three Birds

Jennifer Martin. Age 14. Grade 7
Cowichan Band
Kuper Island Residential School

Third Prize, 1963

The Great Spirit

William Louie. Age 11. Grade 5
Chemainus Band
Kuper Island Residential School

AN UNFINISHED JOURNEY

Bruce McCarthy

Gliding across the sky, a flock of shags, their brown feathers glistening in the sun, waited for two braves to emerge from their hut and bow before them, for the shags were their gods. When at last they appeared, the braves paid homage to the shags and immediately set out to bring the good tidings to the other tribes along Queen Charlotte Strait. The shags had appeared above their village, a sign that a good hunting season was approaching.

As they skimmed the rough waters of Queen Charlotte Strait in their dug-out, a sudden fog closed in around them, blocking their view of the hazardous reefs. Undaunted by the swells of the angry sea, and the heavy mist, the braves gripped their paddles and moved steadily onward. Suddenly, failing to dodge an on-coming wave, their small dug-out was hurled, mercilessly, against the jagged rocks, and as the two braves disappeared into the depths of the sea, the weird cries of the shags up above sounded like the mournful chant of a death hymn. Then, suddenly, something strange happened. The shiny brown feathers of the shags turned to a deadly black. And to this day, the shags wear their black feathers, a symbol of mourning for the lost braves.

THE SPIRIT OF THE OWL

David Henry   Told by his grandmother

I have a grandmother who is one hundred and fifteen.

She is so old that she cannot walk. She is so old that she has also lost her eyesight. She has told me a lot of her Indian stories, and I will never forget some of them. There is one story that I really enjoy the most. She has learned to hear the spirits and to talk to them. Although she is blind she can see these spirits. This is the story.

My great-grandfather was. of course, much older than my grandmother. He had died long before I was brought into this world. This great-grandfather of mine was a famous medicine man. One day an accident occurred. A little child had been attacked by an owl, who had stolen the spirit from the child. The child lay dead and the parents wept in vain to restore its life. They called my great-grandfather in. He came and listened to what had happened.

That night he went out alone into the woods. There they heard him sing and call. After a long time he returned with his head bowed low. He told all to leave the house. They did. Again my great-grandfather danced and sang. Soon a voice joined him. It was the voice of the child. My great-grandfather came out. He addressed everyone around the campfire. He told how he spoke with the owl, and danced for him. Finally he got the child's spirit back. But he had had to bargain with the owl. No child was ever to go outside when the moon was full and large in the sky. with an apple in her hand, for that would be a sign to the owl that he could have the spirit of the child.

Today parents tell this same tale. No Indian child ever eats an apple outside at night time when the moon is full in the sky. My grandmother has spoken to the spirits. The spirits have told her that this is true.

OWLS

Willard Pelkey

Many moons ago the braves were out hunting. They had surrounded a small herd of deer. They used the sounds of birds as signals to close in on the herd. In this way they were able to get food for their tribe.

On another occasion they had just got into the thick part of the woods when they heard a strange sound, one which they had never heard before. They were afraid and ran away except for one. This brave was young and had just become a hunter. As he stood he heard the flapping of strong wings. He turned around but he was too late; the big bird was upon him. He was surrounded by the bird's wings and he himself became an owl. When the braves returned they heard the same strange sound. This time they didn't run. They realized that the sound was their friend trying to talk to them.

To this day we hear owls through the darkness trying to talk to us while we are asleep.

A LESSON TOO LATE

James Short

Chukoop, an Indian boy, lived with his family on a small island off the west coast. He was always very mischievous and delighted in taunting everyone and everything. His wise old grandmother often warned him that unkind deeds would reap their just reward. But Chukoop only laughed and continued his cruel pranks.

One day, Chukoop decided to pick on some crows, so he built a trap and placed a few scraps of fish on the inside. He crouched behind a tree as he waited for the crows to descend. Finally, a few crows landed by the trap. Slowly, they edged their way inside, and at that moment Chukoop pulled the string. He raced to the trap and took out the crows, one by one. As he did so, he plucked out all their feathers. He left their wing feathers on, so that they would be able to fly. Then what a laugh he had as the featherless crows flew away!

Several days later, some old women came to the village where Chukoop lived, and they asked if he would like to pick berries with them. Chukoop chuckled to himself as he thought of giving the old women a scare, so he decided to go along. They walked into the woods, and when they were out of sight, the old women removed their disguises, and there stood the crows from whom Chukoop had taken all the feathers. For the first time in his life, Chukoop was terrified. And, as the crows carried him off, Chukoop remembered his grandmother's warning. Chukoop had reaped his reward.

THE OWL

Floyd Edwards

Indians of long ago were very superstitious. They believed that if you ate any food outside late at night an owl would come down and strike you with one of its wings. They said that if you were hit with one of its wings your chin would go to one side. They said also that if you made toast at night the spirits would come around the house and would make all kinds of strange noises. Some of these spirits were said to make human sounds and to knock at the doors. When the people went to see who was at the door all they could see was the empty darkness.

We have been told that, if at night we walk around by ourselves, an owl will come and wrap its wings around our head. In this way the owl will smother a person to death. But if you carry a stick in your mouth the owl will not come near. Why is the stick supposed to protect you? The owl will be prevented from putting its wings around you.

The early Indians also believed that if they looked outside at night they might see a spirit.

They believed that a person must never make fun of an Indian dancer. If they do they will become sick.

The Indians believed that if they were to sit where a dancer had sat they would get boils.

THE BLACK BIRDS

Richard Thomas

Once, long ago, there was an Indian girl who used to talk all the time. On one particular day a great chief was on his death bed. The witch doctor was singing Indian songs over him and uttering many strange noises. These songs and sounds had an important part in the ceremonies when someone was dying and there was not to be interruption.

Suddenly this girl ran excitedly into the tent and began to talk and talk, quickly and loudly to everyone around her. Suddenly, in the middle of a song, she screamed. At that very instant the chief died.

The witch-doctor was angry and in his anger he turned the girl into a pitch-black bird. To this day her descendants are black and fly in the air and make a great deal of noise. We call these descendants of hers crows.

THE GREEDY OLD RAVEN

Peter Hanson

Long, long ago, there lived an old raven who had a friend who was very slow at eating his food. They used to go to each house and look for food left by other people.

Sometimes they got some food and sometimes they did not get any. When they got some, the raven ate most of the food. His friend got hardly any. On they would go to another house. They did not get any at this next house so they went to where the old raven lived. Here they looked for some food. They were in luck. They found some food in the old raven's house. They started eating the food that they found in his house. The greedy old raven had all the food before his friend was able to get any of it in his mouth. I forgot to tell you that the old raven's friend had a small mouth. That is why he can only eat slowly.

THREE BIRDS

Jennifer Martin   Told by her mother

A long time ago blue jays and all other birds were said to be living persons.

A blue jay suggested, "Why don't we go to pick blackberries?"

"I know where there is a great number of berries," replied Robin.

"Yes, just along the side of the mountain," said Blue Jay.

Crow offered to bring them across the river and back again.

Crow waited by the canoe while they went to pick berries. They were up there all afternoon. When the sun was setting they came down. Then after all the things were in the canoe Crow shouted, "Run, run, the enemy has come. Hide, hide, I will fight him."

They all ran to hide behind and up in the trees. Then instead of fighting the enemy, Crow ate all the berries that were picked. "Help, help," he yelled.

His friends came running and asked if he was all right.

When they got there they were so surprised because Crow was so fat. He had eaten all the berries that were picked.

"Let's leave him here," said Robin.

"Yes, just leave him here. He is so fat he cannot move," replied Blue Jay.

So they gathered all their belongings and got into the canoe and paddled homeward.

That is why Crow is a bird because he was so greedy. He ate so much.

Robin became a bird because he too likes to eat.

Blue Jay became a bird because he is so noisy.

THE GREAT SPIRIT

William Louie

Long ago the Indians believed that certain birds were healing birds. They ate the entrails of this bird because they thought these would cause them to live forever.

The Great Indian Spirit warned them saying, "Do not eat too much or you will get very ill and die."

Many Indians did not obey the Great Spirit and died of sickness. But there was one lad in the tribe who did not eat the entrails of the birds. So the rest of the tribe got very angry with him and killed him. Later the Great Spirit spoke. He said, "You should not have killed him." The Great Spirit was very angry and killed all the birds on the earth.

After a while the Indians were sorry for what they had done and cried, "Spirit, Spirit, save us." They suffered hunger for there were no birds to hunt for food.

Finally the Great Spirit said, "You have suffered enough." So one of the braves went to pray for the return of the birds. He came back in two days followed by many birds. These birds were used as food only.

After this the Indians prayed to the Great Spirit to let them live forever, in his Happy Hunting Grounds.

LEGENDS

The Twin Brothers

Martha Justin, Age 15, Grade 8
Kyuquot Band
Kyuquot Indian Day School
Kyuquot, B.C.

Second Prize, 1964

The Story of Rivers Inlet Hamatcha

Kathleen Lagis, Age 10, Grade 4
Tsawataineuk Band
Kingcome Inlet Indian Day School
Kingcome Inlet, B.C.

First Honourable Mention, 1966

The Nine Sons

Jennifer Martin, Age 15, Grade 8
Cowichan Band
Kuper Island Residential School
Kuper Island, B.C.

The Legend of the Spirit and a Boy

Joan Morris, Age 14, Grade 7
Songhees Band
Kuper Island Residential School

First Honourable Mention, 1963

A Buhkwuss and Three Boys

Lois Elaine Dawson, Age 12, Grade 6
Tsawataineuk Band
Kingcome Inlet Indian Day School

A Fight for Life

Larry Joseph, Age 13, Grade 7
Nootka Band
Wood Elementary School
Port Alberni, B.C.

Jee-Ga-Jo-La the Mighty

Phillip Dawson, Age 15, Grade 7
Tsawataineuk Band
Kingcome Inlet Indian Day School

Thunder Bird

Alice Underwood, Age 16, Grade 8
Tsawout Band
Kuper Island Residential School

Hiptooh

Joyce James, Age 14, Grade 8
Nitinat Band
A. H. Neill Jr. Sr. School
Alberni, B.C.

Third Prize, 1962

Shan-Tec's Cloak

Frances Beltgens, Age 14, Grade 8
No Band given
Kuper Island Residential School

THE TWIN BROTHERS

Martha Justin   Told by her mother

A long time ago, at a place called Walthu, there were two boys who were twins. Their names were Maclauh and Quatin.

One day Maclauh became very ill. They would not let his twin brother see him. The next day their father noticed that his son was dying, so he took Quatin on a trip to look for herring. When they returned, after three days, they found that Maclauh had passed away while they were gone.

Every day Quatin asked the people where they had put Maclauh, but no one would answer him. Finally, after asking everyone, he strolled over to some of the little girls playing dolls together and asked the same question. One of the little girls answered him. "He is in a huge square box up in that tree," she replied pointing to an evergreen tree.

Quatin was satisfied and ran to climb the tree. When he reached the top of the tree, where Maclauh's box was placed he forced the top of the box to open it. After getting it open with an old piece of steel, he climbed in. Suddenly Maclauh spoke. "Is that you my dear brother?" Before Quatin could answer Maclauh spoke again. "I have been waiting very long and I am tired."

Without giving Quatin a chance to answer he shoved his brother inside himself. Then he leaped down from the top of the tall tree. He dashed for the shoreline where a dogfish was waiting. Without waiting to catch his breath, he jumped onto the back of the fish. He grabbed the gills and with his foot he kicked the fish. Immediately the fish began to swim. After a few hours they reached the shoreline of a village which Quatin had never seen before. They got off and the fish swam away.

At the village Maclauh always talked to Quatin, but the people thought he was crazy because they couldn't see Quatin, and yet Maclauh never stopped talking.

One day they went swimming. Not knowing someone had followed them Maclauh released Quatin. The person who saw all this told the others and they all went down to the stream where Maclauh and Quatin were swimming. They told Maclauh to marry one of the women there. The next day he was married.

When the people said Quatin must marry he refused and said that he wanted to go home.

He ran over to a couple of old women and asked where they were going. They answered him, "We are going to your village."

When he asked if he could go along they told him to be there before sunrise the next morning. The next morning, as arranged, Quatin hurried to where the old women were waiting for him. Shortly after they left the wind began to shriek through the air. The canoe rocked back and forth, and for the first time Quatin noticed that each side of the canoe was halfway off, flapping in the wind. One of the women saw that he was afraid, so she covered him with a blanket. When they reached the beach of Walthu, they took the blanket off him and put another blanket on him. The instant the second blanket touched him he became invisible. The old women put on their blankets also.

They went from house to house killing one person in each house. Their first victim was a rich woman. One of the old women, invisible under her blanket, went and sat beside her victim. As soon as the blanket touched the rich woman she let out a shriek and fell down, not moving.

The wealthy husband called the other people to help him put his wife in a box and placed her on top of the tallest tree. Some of the people helped select his wife's useless belongings and the rest were given to his cousin. After the woman's belongings were thrown away the old women took them and put them into their canoe.

They went to another house and told Quatin to do what they had done. So he went and sat beside a young, handsome man. The instant Quatin's blanket touched the young man he also gave a loud cry and died. Of course, the young man's parents grieved for their son. Then the old women took their blanket off Quatin. They said that they wouldn't kill his parents, because he had helped them to kill the people so that they could have the victim's belongings.

The instant the blanket was off Quatin, he became visible again.

When he went into the house he was so happy to see his family, as they were to see him.

Quatin did not tell them where he had been nor what he had done.

THE STORY OF RIVERS INLET HAMATCHA

Kathleen Lagis   Told by Chief Henry Nelson

Nunwa-Kawi had three sons. One had only one leg and used crutches. They were going hunting, and they happened to pass by "The-man-of-roots" who advised them not to go near the smoke that is reddish-coloured, but to go to the white smoke, which resembles mountain goats. Or they could go to the brownish-coloured smoke which is the home of the deer.

Mr. Root gave them oil, a sharp comb, and a stone in case they should happen to go to the house where the smoke is red in colour, for this is the home of Hamatcha, the man-eater. Mr. Root told them to pour the oil on the ground, which will make a big lake so that the man-eater Hamatcha would not catch up to the man who had only one leg. Then the sharp comb would form big jungles, and the stone would be a steep mountain. So they had good advice from Mr. Root.

The three brothers carried on with their journey and with their hunting. One of the brothers got hurt on his knee and the blood ran down his leg. Then the three boys went into the house that did not have any smoke on the fire. The boy started crying, as soon as he saw the blood running down his leg. The one-legged man shot his arrow out of the door, so that they could get out of the house. As soon as they started running for home they met the wife of Hamatcha, shouting for her husband. So the Hamatcha came whistling like lightning. He tried to catch up to the boys, but the oil with which they had made a big lake made the Hamatcha have to go around the lake. When he went that way he nearly caught up to them and so they let the sharp comb fall. This formed jungles. Then Mr. Hamatcha had to go around the jungles. At last he came to where the stone had formed a big mountain. Finally the boys got almost home and they shouted to their father to tighten all the doors, for the Hamatcha was following them. Their father was so excited that when the boys entered the house he locked all the doors. When the Hamatcha arrived he tried to find a place to get into the house, with all his whistling and shouting.

The father of the three brothers invited Hamatcha, and Hamatcha's wife and family for a feast. They were invited again the next day. So the Hamatcha went home. Nunwa-Kawi and his sons worked all night digging a hole behind a plank where the

Hamatcha and his wife and Nunwa-Kawi's sons were to sit for a big feast. They stewed their dog, in preparation for the Hamatcha and his family's arrival. So the one-legged brother hid behind the plank where the hole had been dug, which was about four feet in depth, ready for Hamatcha and his family to fall into. Everything was ready and prepared with excitement for the Hamatcha family.

When they arrived they were welcomed. It was explained that the stew was the son with one leg.

Very shortly after they were seated the one-legged son pulled the pegs from behind the plank and the man-eater Hamatcha and his wife and sons fell into the hole and the three brothers immediately swept fire over the man-eater and his family.

This is the reason mosquitoes like human blood. They are said to be the ashes of Mr. Hamatcha, the man-eater.

THE NINE SONS

Jennifer Martin   Told by her mother

Once there lived a man who married and went to live on a mountain far away. He and his wife lived on this mountain and each year there was another child to add to the family. There were nine boys and one girl. The name of the girl was Enna.

The boys were taught by their father Josia to hunt deer and ducks. Their meat supply was always plentiful.

Enna and Quatsamat, the mother, did all the cooking and everything about the house. In the evening Enna and her mother would go for a walk in the woods.

One evening Enna went for a walk alone. Her brothers and her father were out hunting. Enna took an unusual trail this time. On this trail, not far from her home she met a man. He was very unusual. He looked almost like a rock. Enna asked, "What are you chewing?"

The man's answer was, "I chew pitch for gum."

"Oh," replied Enna, "I have never tasted that before. Would you show me where you got it?"

"It is near to the river's bank, not far from here," the man told her.

They had gone quite far when Enna became frightened. She

100

pulled the strings on her shawl and laid them on the branches that she could reach.

As they came around the bend Enna sighted a river. "Is this where you got your gum?" asked Enna.

"Yes," the man told her, "over by that tree."

When Enna had got some gum the man asked her if she wanted a boat ride. Enna consented.

By this time her brothers were looking for her. They had split up at the trail.

The group of four boys saw the pieces of string on the branches alongside of the trail. One of them said, "We have found where she has gone."

At the river they had an unexpected attacker. All the brothers turned to fight but the stranger was upon them before they could attack. When they were all unconscious the man ripped from under the collar bone of each and took out the heart. As he was taking the hearts out he ate every one.

When the mother of these boys found out she wept at the place where the bodies were found. Each day she came to this place, and here she cried, and her tears mixed with the earth and soon formed a ball of earth.

Then one day a very strange thing happened. The ball started to take the shape of a boy. It began to move and to cry. Quatsamat was frightened. But she was happy and she said, "I'll take care of this boy." She brought it up as her own son. His name was Simon.

Simon was growing fast. At the age of one year his height was the height of a two-year-old.

Simon's mother would cry each day for the loss of her sons. One day Simon asked his mother why she was crying.

She told him the sad story while he listened carefully.

At the age of three the boy was man-sized. So he went to seek his brothers. He found the bodies and laid them on the ground.

He was washing the brothers when a rock-like man attacked him. But Simon killed him. He did to him what he had done to the brothers. He opened his chest. There he saw the hearts of his three brothers encircling the heart of the man. Simon took each heart out and placed it into the chest of each brother. Just one heart was ruined, so he used the heart of the rock-like man. Simon splashed his brothers nine times with buckets of water. After which they all came to life.

Simon also brought back Enna, who was working as a slave for the man.

They were all happy and to this day the Cowichan tribe tell how they were saved from the rock-man.

THE LEGEND OF THE SPIRIT AND A BOY

Joan Morris   Told by her grandmother

This took place three and a half miles from Oak Bay. Oak Bay is about two miles from Victoria.

The names of the islands in the story are Discovery and Chatham.

On Discovery lived an old, old lady with the tribe and her only son whom they called Leaping Deer. Her people were not doing well because food was scarce. They barely got enough to eat. They were greatly tempted to leave Discovery Island and move to Chatham.

Later an incident took place which displeased the people and they moved away leaving the young brave alone on the island.

The boy went out into the forest every day when it was time to eat, so finally the Chief with two of his finest braves followed the boy to find out what he was doing.

When Leaping Deer set out the braves followed him at a distance, keeping well out of sight.

Finally, being a distance away from camp, Leaping Deer made a fire and took some dried fish and other foods from where he had stored them in a clump of bushes. Then he started eating. After he had cleaned up the bones and the fire he went to sleep.

The braves started back to camp and when they got there they reported what they had seen happen. The Chief and the people were angry, all except his mother. She wondered what they could do about it. Then the Chief ordered them to start packing and to be ready by the time the sun was ready to set. Everyone started right away. They were all excited. Everyone except Leaping Deer's mother. She did not want to leave her only son alone on the island to starve or to be a victim of whatever harm might come to him. But the people started packing her things no matter what she said. Then they started putting their things in their canoes.

Before his mother got in the canoe she instructed a female

dog to care for the boy when he got back. She was to try to attract his attention to where the food and the fire were. She told the dog that the fire was buried in a clam shell. The dog barked in reply. The reason why the mother left the fire is because fire was hard to obtain. They had to work for hours before they could obtain it.

Just as she finished instructing the dog, it was time to leave. Sorrowfully the mother got into the canoe and was off.

The boy woke up, stretched himself and thought to himself that he had better hurry home before his mother was worried. He started back but when he got near to the camp, he wondered why it was so quiet. So he walked faster. What a sorry-looking sight it was when he got there. Everywhere he looked it was deserted, no one to talk to, nor to joke with. He almost wept with relief when he felt something tugging at his legs. He looked down and saw the little dog. He thought that she was just trying to play with him, so he did not pay any attention to her. But the dog would not leave him alone. Then he realized that the dog was trying to tell him something. So he responded to her little tugs and started following. She commenced digging. He joined in and pretty soon he found the food and the fire.

For many months he was alone with the dog and the other animals that roamed through the forest.

During this time, as he didn't have a blanket, he had to sleep near the fire or in big logs, so he started making a blanket out of bird's feathers. Each day he shot the birds until finally he had collected enough feathers so that the blanket covered him and kept him warm.

One day while he was asleep, he awakened to hear a thud on the ground, like the sound of a person falling or jumping. He did not look up for he was much afraid.

While he lay motionless he heard a loud clear voice say to him in his own language, "Look up, I am not an evil person, I will not harm you."

Slowly the young brave pulled the blanket down from his head and tried to look at the man but he could not make him out for the person seemed to have brightness greater even than that of the sun.

Then the man spoke again, saying, "For many days I have looked down while you were making this blanket. I like it very much and I am wondering if you will give it to me?"

Leaping Deer replied, "I would gladly give it to you but I haven't got any other blanket to use."

So the stranger produced a skin such as is not seen nowadays, and said to him, "I will give you this skin, which will be of more use to you. It will keep you warm and when you want food, just take the tip of it, dip it in the water in the ditch and move it back and forth four times. But before you do this you must dig a clean ditch."

The boy agreed and he took the skin and gave the man his feather blanket. As he did so he asked, "Who are you and where do you come from?"

The stranger replied, "I am a spirit from above. Because of your generosity I will take you back to your own people."

The Spirit was true to his word. Leaping Deer found his family and relatives. They accepted him again as one of their own.

Leaping Deer made use of the skin which he got. He shared the food he was able to get with it. Soon he became one of the most wise and skilful of chiefs.

A BUHKWUSS AND THREE BOYS

Lois Elaine Dawson   Told by her grandfather

My grandfather told me that there were three boys who were playing soccer one evening after supper. All of a sudden one boy said, "Look, I see something behind that log. Do you see it? Let's go and see what it is."

The other boy said, "No, lets not go and see what it is. It might be a bear or a wolf, and besides it is getting dark now. We should go home." The other boy said, "If you are afraid, you stay here and wait for us." And he and his friend went to see what it was.

Just at the moment they got to the end of the log, a big hairy man jumped out from behind the log. He was big and tall. (In our language he is called "buhkwuss" and in English he is "The Wildman".) He put those two boys in his basket and started to hurry towards his cave in the woods.

My grandfather said that luckily it happened that one of the boys had a hunting knife with him. They cut a hole in the basket, big enough for a boy to get through. Then they fell out one by one and ran like the wind to the field where they had been playing. When they got to the field they saw the other boy waiting for them.

When the two boys reached the other boy, this boy asked, "What was that?" The two boys told a lie to him and said, "It was just an old black jacket that someone must have lost." When they told that lie my grandfather said that their noses grew longer. And with each lie their noses grew more. They wondered why their noses grew. Each asked his father and were told that this happens to people who tell lies. It must have taught them a good lesson!

When the old "buhkwuss" got to his cave he put the basket down. Then he made a nice hot fire. When he went to get his basket he wondered why it was so light. He looked into it and cried, "Oh, no! They have all got away. What will I do without any food?" So he just sat down and starved to death.

That was the end of the big bad "buhkwuss".

A FIGHT FOR LIFE

Larry Joseph   Told by his father

Once there were two young Indian boys who everyone honoured because they were the two fastest runners in the village. If the people wanted food, they would send the two boys out to get some. The way they caught a deer was by running as fast as they could, jumping on the deer and killing it with a knife.

One day when they were chasing a deer, it got cornered at the edge of a cliff. The two boys continued to run after it with their knives, ready to kill. The deer ran and jumped over the cliff rather than be caught. The boys went to look for it. It had fallen to a ledge below.

On the ledge there was a cave and outside of it piles of bones could be seen. Growls of an unknown animal could be heard from within the cave. The boys shivered at the sound of it. As they watched what would happen, a huge beast came crashing out. The boys jumped back in fright. When it saw the deer it picked it up and carried it into the cave as if it were a sack of feathers.

Leaving the deer inside the cave the beast came back, onto the ledge, grunting and growling. It began to sniff the air, for it had picked up the scent of the two Indian boys. Immediately it spotted the boys it darted up the cliff with amazing speed. The boys ran off as fast as they could go but unfortunately the beast began to gain on them.

As one of the boys was dashing through the thicket a piece of his jacket was ripped off and it fell in the path of the beast. As soon as the beast spotted the piece of torn jacket it picked it up, sniffed it, ripped it, and threw it onto the ground stamping upon it with great fury. While it was doing this the two boys were running for their lives.

The boy who had his jacket ripped was smart enough to throw another piece of deer-skin jacket and the beast did the same thing over again. While it was doing this the boys were running as fast as they could go. This was repeated over and over, until finally the two boys reached a river where they had left their canoe. Out of breath they jumped into their canoe and pushed to the middle of the river.

Strangely the beast stopped right at the edge of the water. It backed up, then charged towards the water with speed greater than that of the boys. Again, right at the edge of the water it stopped short. Back it went to try again, but again the same thing happened. Finally as the beast jumped it touched the top of the water. As soon as it did, it turned into a pile of foam.

Just to make sure that the beast was no longer there one of the boys fired an arrow into the foam but nothing was there.

But the animals around continued to be afraid of the foam that gathers at the water's edge. That is why sea birds never swim into the foam, they go all the way around to continue on their way.

JEE-GA-JO-LA THE MIGHTY

Phillip Dawson

There was a man named Jee-Ga-Jo-La who wanted to become strong, so he went down to the beach at night to bathe. He believed that the cold water would make him strong. One night while he was in the water a man came to him out of the river. Jee-Ga-Jo-La did not realize that he had company until the man came out of the river and spoke to Jee-Ga-Jo-La, asking him what he was doing.

Jee-Ga-Jo-La told the man that he was bathing so that he might become strong. The man breathed on Jee-Ga-Jo-La to give him strength. Then the man said, "Get a rock, then squeeze it until the water starts dripping out." The first time it did not work. The man breathed on him again and told him to squeeze the rock again. This time it worked. The water dripped out of the rock. Then the man said to Jee-Ga-Jo-La, "Now you are a strong man, as you wished that you would be."

The very next day Jee-Ga-Jo-La and the other people of the village saw a bear coming up the river. The men wished to kill it, but all the canoes were dried up. All the men got together to push the canoes into the water, but they couldn't move any of them. Jee-Ga-Jo-La saw them pulling and straining and he went down to help. He wished to show his strength. So he went to the bow of one of the canoes. It is said that he just grabbed the rope and pulled the canoe into the water. Now when the men saw it they all admired him. Then they all got on one canoe with Jee-Ga-Jo-La in the bow so that he could throw a spear at the bear, but when they got near the bear Jee-Ga-Jo-La jumped on its back. He tore the bear right in half. He threw one half of the bear onto the boat. All the men were so scared that they jumped off the canoe into the river.

All the men talked about the strength of Jee-Ga-Jo-La. He was known all along the west coast.

THUNDER BIRD

Alice Underwood   Told by her grandfather

I heard the Indians chanting. I wondered. Then my grandfather told me this story.

There once lived a mighty chief, Thunder Bird. They say he would often leave the village for a day. When he returned he would chant to the Spirit of the Thunder Bird. When the Thunder Bird heard the cry of the mighty chief it came down with a flash and left the clouds with a cracking noise. The villagers were frightened. Chief Thunder Bird told them it was the Spirit that had come to visit. They all came out of their houses. The babies cried for fear. Again the chief chanted. Rain came down. It is said the Thunder Bird was weeping for the people when he saw how hungry and frightened they were. His tears filled the rivers and watered the lands and helped the fruit to grow.

This changed the village. Chief Thunder Bird gathered his tribe to thank the Great Spirit. The babies and women and the braves were in their finest clothes. The mighty chief came from his house in the grandest of his robes, which had many strange designs on it, and he was wearing the head dress which he had started to make when he was a young brave. Many feathers were on the head dress.

The people wondered why there were many-coloured feathers which stood out from the others. All they could do was wonder for as yet they had no explanation.

The chief told them how he had collected the feathers, but when they asked about the many-coloured feathers he only looked at them with great pleasure and did not answer their questions.

Many moons passed. These people who were once happy and full of laughter were now sad, for they had seen many strange things in the moon that had passed. Now again they saw a strange happening. The chief was growing white. The people heard the chant get louder. It echoed in the valley. Everyone joined in. While they sang the chief danced to his house. This dance was the death dance. He came out with a dancing stick, bow and arrow and many things that he had fought for. He gave them away.

He stopped the chant and said, "You wonder how Chief Thunder Bird won the many-coloured feathers? The Spirit of the Thunder Bird calls me to be the next honoured. But these feathers stay among my people always."

Chief Thunder Bird returned to his house and again the lonely chant started. The lightning came down. Great clouds covered the village. There was another loud noise. The chant slowly died, away. When it died away the great clouds were lifted.

All ran to the chief's house. But just the many-coloured feathers remained. Chief Thunder Bird was now the Powerful One.

Whenever Chief Thunder Bird comes down to earth he uses the clouds to hide himself.

Whenever it thunders and the lightning flashes across the sky. it reminds me of the story and I can hear the chant. "O Wise One. help my people. Be with them. Never lose love for these helpless ones. Give them strength in warfare. O Mighty One. stay with us."

HIPTOOH

Joyce Thomas   Told by her grandmother

The old chief Hiptooh arrived at the end of the trail just as the red sun sank behind the mountains. Must he go on? He stood there at the crossroad to the "Coora-Mya" or "Forbidden Garden" and considered only for a minute. Yes. for the sake of his loved ones back at the village who were starving and had been doing so for the past week, he had to go on. It was all because the rough waters were coming in fast, but bringing no fish for food. The hunters also had returned empty-handed from hunting trips. He must go on.

Total darkness reigned as he stumbled along the bushy trail which was about two-and-a-half feet in width with sharp branches jutting out and poking at him. In the far distance he could hear an owl as it hooted softly and eerily. Otherwise it was quiet, much too quiet for Hiptooh's comfort.

Then he saw it, "Suka-Sout" or the crooked stump which marked the end of the safe trail. Beyond that lay the mystery place to which all his fathers and grandfathers and their fathers before them had gone. None of them had ever returned. With this knowledge the fear grew deep down in the heart of Hiptooh. but the fear was pushed away by the desire to prove himself a great chief. Back at the village though. the eyes of all the people gazed on him with admiration and respect for his skill at hunting the deer and spearing the great fish.

His thoughts were suddenly interrupted by the sound of slow. steady drums which had the definite ring of death! Hiptooh tried vainly to peer into the darkness but the strain was too much for his weary eyes. His senses seemed to be leaving him completely.

He was only vaguely aware of soft spiderweb-like material brushing against his cheeks and bare arms.

He shrank back in horror at the sight which next met his eyes. But no sound escaped his dry lips. The drums were louder and faster now, but he was only aware of the thing wavering slowly toward him. It had a head, a mass of flesh and blood, with white stringy hair matted into it, while one eye dangled helplessly from a blood-dripping forehead. Its walk was unsteady as it supported its wispy body on a long white cane.

With a sigh Hiptooh sank to the ground and the last words he heard were, "You have earned your reward. Your people shall eat." The rolling drums stopped and once more peace settled over the graveyard.

SHAN-TEC'S CLOAK

Frances Beltgens

Shan-tec was a boy who lived many ages ago. Shan-tec means "boasting one," and indeed he did boast often. One day, as he was playing with his playmates, he pointed to the jagged peak of Octlet-nan, (now known as Mount Tzouhalem) behind the village and said, "I bet I can climb to the top of that peak." His playmates laughed, but his father said to him, "Take your cloak and go. When you get to the top, hang your cloak there so we all can see." Shan-tec tried to say that he was only fooling, but his father spoke sternly.

When he came to the edge of the forest he met his friend the bear. The bear carried him across the river and up the sloped part of the mountain. Then when the bear could no longer proceed he met his friend, the sure-footed mountain deer. The deer carried him up the steep face of the mountain, to the very top.

Here they both rested and ate the berries that grew there. Then Shan-tec went to the edge of the peak and hung his cloak upon it. He looked down upon the village that seemed so small. Then he turned, and upon the deer's back he went down the mountain, until they met the bear. Shan-tec had gathered berries on the cliff and gave them to the bear, who carried him again to the edge of the forest. From there he went alone into the village. The people of the village had already seen his cloak and congratulated him warmly.

And even to this day in the evening when the sun goes down and shines upon the peak, people see a red spot there, and say it is Shan-tec's cloak that still hangs there.

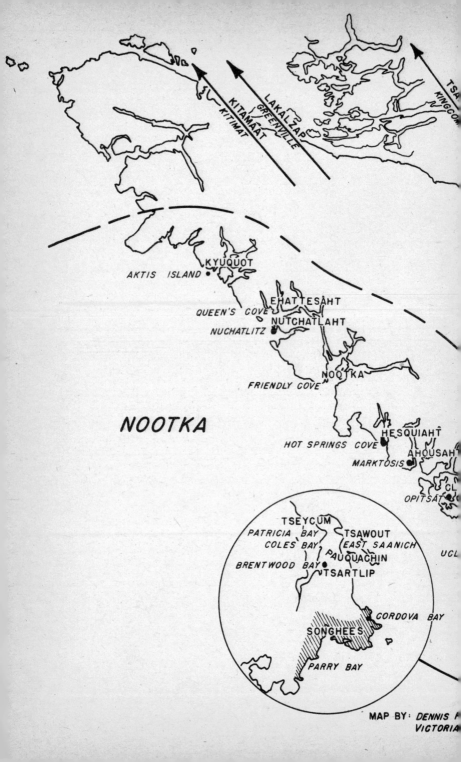

KITIMAT
KITAMAAT
GREENVILLE
LAKALZAP
KINGCOM
TSA

KYUQUOT
AKTIS ISLAND

EHATTESAHT
QUEEN'S COVE
NUTCHATLAHT
NUCHATLITZ

NOOTKA
FRIENDLY COVE

NOOTKA

HESQUIAHT
HOT SPRINGS COVE
AHOUSAH
MARKTOSIS
CL
OPITSAT

TSEYCUM
PATRICIA BAY
TSAWOUT
COLES BAY
EAST SAANICH
PAUQUACHIN
BRENTWOOD BAY
TSARTLIP
UCL

CORDOVA BAY
SONGHEES
PARRY BAY

MAP BY: DENNIS
VICTORIA

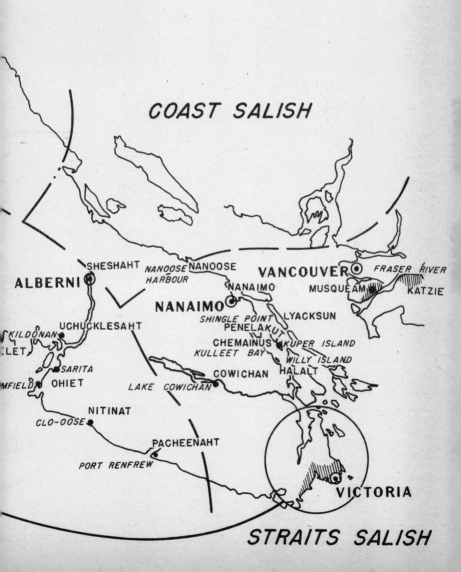

COAST SALISH

SHESHAHT   NANOOSE NANOOSE   VANCOUVER   FRASER RIVER
ALBERNI   HARBOUR   NANAIMO   MUSQUEAM   KATZIE
                                    NANAIMO
UCHUCKLESAHT   SHINGLE POINT   LYACKSUN
KILDONAN   PENELAKUT
LET)   CHEMAINUS   KUPER ISLAND
        SARITA   KULLEET BAY   WILLY ISLAND
MFIELD OHIET   HALALT
        LAKE COWICHAN   COWICHAN
        NITINAT
CLO-OOSE
        PACHEENAHT
PORT RENFREW   VICTORIA

STRAITS SALISH